VOLUM

Mere Christianity

Pilgrim's Progress

The Brothers Karamazov

The Imitation of Christ

A Taste of the Classics

SUMMARIZED BY KENNETH D. BOA

Biblica™

Biblica Publishing
We welcome your questions and comments.

USA   1820 Jet Stream Drive, Colorado Springs, CO 80921
        www.authenticbooks.com
India   Logos Bhavan, Medchal Road, Jeedimetla Village, Secunderabad
        500 055, A.P.

A Taste of the Classics, Volume One
ISBN-13: 978-1-93406-810-6

12 11 10 / 6 5 4 3 2 1

Published in 2010 by Biblica

Scripture quotations are taken from the NEW AMERICAN STANDARD BIBLE®, Copyright © 1960, 1962, 1963, 1968, 1971, 1972, 1973, 1975, 1977, 1995 by The Lockman Foundation. Used by permission.

A catalog record for this book is available through the Library of Congress.

Printed in the United States of America

CONTENTS

PREFACE

Christians have a rich heritage of devout saints and brilliant thinkers, many of whom have left us their writings. Those with access to these writings have a treasure trove to help them along their journey of faith.

However, many of us lead frenetic lives that don't leave time for reflection, let alone engagement with some of the best Christian literature from across the generations. Dr. Kenneth Boa has helpfully summarized a number of these classics to give you a taste of what you may be missing. You may find deep refreshment in this book. Or, as with any sampler platter, you may discover a morsel you would delight to savor again. Perhaps you could then pick up the original work with a framework already in place to help you immediately engage the classic. Regardless of how you use this book, we hope your faith will be enriched through the considerable insights of generations before us.

A note on method: Dr. Boa cites numerous passages from each book. Because he proceeds through a book from beginning to end, we have chosen not to cite page numbers. This will create a more pleasant reading experience for you, and you will be able to locate passages from each book by the cues the author gives here.

Since the primary audience for this book is American, we have changed spellings to what is commonly accepted in the United States. However, we have left the original style and capitalization for each author. There are some points where authors used dubious capitalization, but we have chosen not to note them (using [sic]), again for ease of reading. Poetry is usually set in prose, for the sake of space. In this case, the initial capital letter in a line of poetry has been lowercased. The following editions are cited in this book:

Lewis, C. S. *Mere Christianity*. New York: HarperSanFrancisco, 2001.

Bunyan, John. *The Pilgrim's Progress*. New York: Signet Classics, 2009.

Dostoyevsky, Fyodor. *The Brothers Karamazov*, trans. David McDuff. London: Penguin Classics, 2003.

à Kempis, Thomas. *The Imitation of Christ*, trans. William C. Creasy. Notre Dame, IN: Ave Maria Press, 1989.

Special thanks are due to Cindy Barnwell, who helped Dr. Boa edit and enrich the manuscript for publication.

Mere Christianity

Introduction

The material contained in C. S. Lewis's *Mere Christianity* was originally a series of radio messages that was aired by British Broadcasting Corporation during the Second World War. His first broadcasts included *The Case for Christianity* and *Christian Behavior*. These were aired in 1943, and *Beyond Personality* was heard in 1945. These three works were combined later into the book *Mere Christianity*.

By the term "mere Christianity" Lewis referred to the essence of Christianity rather than to its denominational manifestations. The term implies that there are particular biblical doctrines that distinguish Christianity. Lewis dealt with basic, creedal orthodoxy—those essential elements revealed in Scripture and condensed in the great affirmations of the Apostles' Creed and the Nicene Creed. Lewis sought to delineate those beliefs that Christians share in common—the essentials of the faith. His *Mere Christianity* reflects the spirit of the famous statement: "In the essentials, unity; in the nonessentials, diversity; and in all things, charity."

Lewis introduced his work with an image of a hallway containing numerous doors leading into various rooms. He explained, "If I can bring anyone into that hall, I shall have done what I attempted. But it is in the rooms, not in the hall, that there are fires and chairs and meals. The hall is a place to wait in, a place from which to try the various doors, not a place to live in." In other words, he argued that all believers in Christ can share the hall, but eventually each must discern which community's door he or she will enter. Lewis understood the biblical emphasis on unity within the true church, for he warned, "When you have reached your own room, be kind to those who have chosen different doors and to those who are still in the hall. If they are wrong, they need your prayers all the more; and if they are your enemies, then you are under orders to pray for them. That is one of the rules common to the whole house." This admonition is in keeping with Paul's in Romans 15:5–6: "Now may the God who gives perseverance and encouragement grant you to be of the same mind with one another according to Christ Jesus, so that with one accord you may with one voice glorify the

God and Father of our Lord Jesus Christ."

Following this analogy, Lewis explored the moral sensibility that humans ought to possess. If we quarrel, if we praise, or if we blame, he asserted, we are appealing to some moral "ought"—to some standard that necessitates a divine lawgiver. Having established an argument for the existence of God and absolute law/morality, he continued in an exploration of competing conceptions of God, distinguishing between who God is and is not and establishing a case for the authenticity of Christ. He then examined the implications of God's moral standards for our lives and the fundamentals of Christian behavior.

In another section of the work, Lewis addressed the doctrine of the Trinity. He demonstrated that the life of God is really a Trinitarian life—a fellowship and unity among the Father, Son, and Spirit. He argued that the love present within the Trinity is the love that believers are called to share and enjoy. He asserted that the spiritual life is really the embracing of a new life in Christ, which makes us new people with a divine ability to grow in holiness. He focused on these concepts and then drew some powerful applications at the end.

So, let's take a look at some of this material. The first two parts are the most difficult because Lewis explored philosophical and theological concepts. I will provide just an overview of these two sections in order to offer an idea of the complete work.

The Law of Human Nature

In the chapter on human nature, Lewis addressed the law of nature itself, and he referred to one of his other books, *The Abolition of Man*, which was published in 1940. In essence it argues that all religions and cultures share a common morality—what Lewis called the "Tao." Lewis noted that across time periods, cultures, and continents, people seemed to espouse very similar values. He explained, "Think of a country where people were admired for running away in battle, or where a man felt proud of double-crossing all the people who had been kindest to him. You might as well try to imagine a country where two and two made five." There are certain values that all cultures embrace, and this is part of what it means to be human. Lewis went on to say, "Whenever you find a man who says he does not believe in a real Right and Wrong, you will find the same man going back on this a moment later. He may break his promise to you, but if you try breaking one to him he will be complaining 'It's not fair.'" The fact that we quarrel and recognize injustice and unfairness in others is an indication that a true standard of goodness or fairness exists.

Lewis examined the human condition and appealed to humanity's common recognition of morality: "How would you like it if someone did the same to you?" "That's my seat; I was here first." "Leave him alone; he isn't doing you any harm." "Give me some of your orange; I gave you some of mine." "Come on; you promised." Each of these appeals to some instinct, social contract, or obligation; each is an appeal to something we believe is right or wrong.

As Lewis developed this theme, he suggested that the problem was that "this year, or this month, or, more likely, this very day, we have failed to practice ourselves the kind of behavior we expect from other people." It doesn't take divine revelation to show us that we do have a conscience that often condemns us when we discover that we, in fact, violate our own moral standards. We say we ought to treat people with kindness, dignity, and respect, and then we go on and treat people who may be the closest to us in a way that is often more cruel than the way we would treat mere strangers. Why is that? Why is it that we say one thing and do another? Ovid's *Metamorphoses* (circa AD 8) notes the same concept: "I see the better way, and I approve it, while I pursue the worse" (trans. Charles Martin [New York: W. W. Norton & Company, 2005], 224). Often we find ourselves doing that which we don't wish to do. A theme in the writings of essayist Samuel Johnson (1709–1784) concurs: There is that in ourselves which we would not tell our dearest friends. Even the apostle Paul recorded the moral tension he struggled with: "For what I am doing, I do not understand; for I am not practicing what I would like to do, but I am doing the very thing I hate" (Romans 7:15).

Lewis asserted that excuses for our moral failings "are one more proof of how deeply, whether we like it or not, we believe in the Law of Nature. If we do not believe in decent behavior, why should we be so anxious to make excuses for not having behaved decently? . . . For you notice that it is only for our bad behavior that we find all of these explanations. It is only our bad temper that we put down to being tired or worried or hungry; we put our good temper down to ourselves." Paul's statement in Romans 7:16 parallels Lewis's observation: "But if I do the very thing I do not want to do, I agree with the Law, confessing that the Law is good." With his arguments, Lewis asserted that one of the essentials of Christianity is the acknowledgment that humans are, indeed, sinful and aware of their sin. Furthermore, knowledge of sin implies that a discernable standard of right or good exists.

Next Lewis tackled the fallacy that morality is nothing more than a herd instinct. He argued that, in fact, we are often motivated to pursue things that are not instinctual at all. For example, there are times when we do what is both impractical and detrimental to ourselves. In war, soldiers subdue instinct in favor of patriotism. People often suppress fear in order to save others who are in danger. Contrary to assertions that morality is merely a facet of instinct, Lewis demonstrated that our choices are often not our primary impulses and that we find ourselves knowing that something contrary to instinct is the better course of action. He also disproved the idea that morality is mere social convention and argued that if we reduce morality to that level, then by what measure would we be able to judge whether one culture is better than another? Of course, the problem we would have then is that if it were just decent behavior that a nation happens to approve, then there would be no sense in saying that any one nation had ever been more correct in its approval than any other. There is no sense in saying that the world could ever grow morally better or morally worse. Yet we know that is not the way humans actually operate.

He continued to develop the idea that the law of human nature is undeniable. One of the ways we can learn about ourselves is to look inside and see what is there. "The only packet I am allowed to open," he wrote, "is Man. When I do, especially when I open that particular man called Myself, I find that I do not exist on my own, that I am under a law; that somebody or something wants me to behave in a certain way."

Lewis then went on to discuss the contrast between human nature and what he called a materialist philosophy because there are, indeed, two basic ways of looking at this. He addressed the materialist view and contrasted it with the religious. From a materialist perspective, we would have to consider how humans arrived at the idea of morality. Logically, such a view would have to reduce morality to mere instinctual survival. As Lewis noted, "People who take that view think that matter and space just happen to exist, and always have existed, nobody knows why; and that the matter, behaving in certain fixed ways, has just happened, by a sort of fluke, to produce creatures like ourselves who are able to think." Yet a problem quickly arises. Science observes external realities, but, as Lewis pointed out, "we do not merely observe men, we *are* men. In this case we have, so to speak, inside information. . . . Anyone studying Man from the outside as we study electricity or cabbages, not knowing our language and consequently not able to get any inside knowledge from us, but merely observing what we did, would never get the slightest evidence that we had this moral law. How could he? for his observations would only show what we did, and the moral law is about what we ought to do." But, Lewis argued, there is something within us that seems to contradict this limited notion. He posited, "If there was a controlling power outside the universe, it could not show itself to us as one of the facts inside the universe—no more than the architect of a house could actually be a wall or staircase or fireplace in that house. The only way in which we could expect it to show itself would be inside ourselves as an influence or a command trying to get us to behave in a certain way. And that is just what we do find inside ourselves." Lewis argued that while the rest of matter merely obeys the laws of its nature, human beings feel a compulsion to obey "the law of human nature. . . . Something . . . is directing the universe, and . . . appears in me as a law urging me to do right and making me feel responsible and uncomfortable when I do wrong."

Lewis then noted that there is another view of morality that falls in between the materialist and religious views. Lewis called this the "Life-Force philosophy," also known as "Creative Evolution" or "Emergent Evolution." He criticized this Life-Force philosophy—an impersonal, vaguely spiritual force without any personality. He suggested, "One reason why many people find Creative Evolution so attractive is that it gives one much of the emotional comfort of believing in God and none of the less pleasant consequences. . . . The Life-Force is a sort of tame God. You can switch it on when you want, but it will not bother you. All the thrills of religion and none of the cost. Is the Life-Force the greatest achievement of wishful thinking the world has yet seen?"

I might translate this concept into a New Age philosophy of some impersonal element, whether it is higher vibrations or consciousness or something else. However, if it is not personal, it is not something that can fully account for the idea of morality. We cannot, for example, sin against an impersonal object. If we kick someone's car door, we don't ask the car for forgiveness. The owner of the car would be the one to approach. Both the materialist view and the Life-Force view attempt to explain morality apart from accountability. They would both release human beings from guilt and uneasiness due to moral downfalls. Lewis, however, developed this a little further and then noted, "We have cause to be uneasy." Indeed, we have cause to be uneasy because God is personal and holds us personally accountable for our behavior. The natural moral law within us all indicates the existence of a moral God. Lewis logically asserts, "If [the power behind the moral law] is pure impersonal mind, there may be no sense in asking it to make allowances for you or let you off, just as there is no sense in asking the multiplication table to let you off when you do your sums wrong. . . . And it is no use either saying that if there is a God . . . then you do not like Him and are not going to bother about Him. For the trouble is that one part of you is on His side and really agrees with his disapproval of human greed and trickery and exploitation." He goes on to demonstrate "unless the power behind the world really and unalterably detests that sort of behavior, then He cannot be good. On the other hand, we know that if there does exist an absolute goodness it must hate most of what we do. This is the terrible fix we are in. If the universe is not governed by an absolute goodness, then all our efforts are in the long run hopeless. But if it is, then we are making ourselves enemies to that goodness every day."

After presenting these views, Lewis arrived at the heart of his argument in book 1. He explained,

> Christianity simply does not make sense until you have faced the sort of facts I have been describing. . . . It is after you have realized that there is a real Moral Law, and a Power behind the law, and that you have broken that law and put yourself wrong with that Power—it is after all this, and not a moment sooner, that Christianity begins to talk. When you know you are sick, you will listen to the doctor. When you have realized that our position is nearly desperate you will begin to understand what the Christians are talking about. They offer an explanation of how we got into our present state of both hating goodness and loving it. . . . They tell you how the demands of this law, which you and I cannot meet, have

been met on our behalf, how God Himself becomes a man to save man from the disapproval of God.

In summary, the thesis of book 1 is that human awareness of goodness, justice, and fairness, as well as our own failings in those areas, provides the evidence that a personal and good God exists.

Rival Conceptions of God

Book 2 of *Mere Christianity* focuses on what Christians believe. Lewis began with a presentation of the rival concepts regarding God, and he observed that a majority of people "believe in some kind of God or gods." However, people disagree on the sort of God they believe in. Some of them have the idea that God is fundamentally good and define "good" as being what God is like. Others think that God is beyond good and evil. Pantheists, for example, would say that God is everything and that the whole world is a self-expression of his nature. For them, good and evil are only illusions caused by our relative perspective, and ultimately all things that exist constitute one unity. Lewis asserted that if you do not take the distinction between good and bad very seriously, then it is easy to say that anything you find in this world is a part of God. But, of course, if you think some things are really bad, and God is really good, then you cannot talk that way. You must believe that God is separate from the world and that some of the things we see in it are contrary to his will.

This then introduces another issue—the issue of justice in relation to God. If a good God made the world, why does it go wrong? If God created the world, why is it so full of injustice and cruelty? Why does it seem so distorted? Lewis had struggled with the problem of evil before coming to faith in Christ. He revealed the process that he himself went through on his journey from atheism to faith. He wrote, "Of course I could have given up my idea of justice by saying it was nothing but a private idea of my own." In other words, why be so concerned with justice if ultimate reality is so impersonal?

If we stop and think about it, what is the source of justice? If I am a materialist, then the idea of justice isn't contextualized. Regarding this, Lewis observed, "But if I did [claim that justice was a personal concept], then my argument against God collapsed too—for the argument depended on saying that the world was really unjust, not simply that it did not happen to please my fancies." As soon as I speak about the world as being evil, I am appealing to some kind of standard that isn't really cultural conditioning, but is really wrong. Lewis admitted that he greatly struggled with this issue: "My argument against God was that the universe seemed so cruel and unjust. But how had I got this idea of *just* and *unjust*? A man does not call a line crooked unless he has some idea of a straight line. What was I comparing this universe with when I called it unjust?"

He continued, "Thus in the very act of trying to prove that God did not exist—in other words, that the whole of reality was senseless—I found I was forced to assume that one part of reality—namely my idea of justice—was full of sense. Consequently," he concluded, "atheism turns out to be too simple. If the whole universe has no meaning, we should never have found out that it has no meaning; just as, if there were no light in the universe and therefore no creatures with eyes, we should never know it was dark. *Dark* would be a word without meaning." With these arguments, Lewis concluded that he must reject both the atheistic view and the pantheistic belief in an impersonal God or force. Only a personal, good, and righteous God could account for his awareness of justice and injustice.

Invasion of Christ

In the next section of book 2, Lewis noted an important and surprising distinction of Christianity. The concept of evil is a uniquely Christian concept: evil really does exist, and evil is a distortion of the good. Rather than saying that good and evil do not exist, or that they can be blended into nothingness, he was explaining that we all understand that there are some things that are right and other things that are wrong. Lewis was alluding to the Augustinian notion that evil is not a thing in itself but a parasite on the good. Elsewhere he referred to evil as "bent" good, inferring that we must misappropriate or pervert God's good gifts to commit evil, for evil is not original. Lewis developed this argument by looking at things like sexual perversion and cruelty and showed how the badness consists in pursuing good things by the wrong method or in excess: "I do not mean, of course, that the people who do this are not desperately wicked. I do mean that wickedness, when you examine it, turns out to be the pursuit of some good in the wrong way. You can be good for the mere sake of goodness; you cannot be bad for the mere sake of badness." Even when you do something sadistic, there is a pleasure that you are trying to achieve. There is some good that you are trying to accomplish.

Power and wealth, for example, are not intrinsically evil, but the means by which people pursue them can result in evil. Perhaps more clearly, Lewis explained it this way: "To be bad, [one] must exist, and have intelligence and will." (Here he was, of course, speaking theoretically.) "But existence, intelligence and will are in themselves good. Therefore he must be getting them from the Good Power: even to be bad he must borrow or steal from his opponent. And do you now begin to see why Christianity has always said that the devil is a fallen angel? That is not a mere story for the children. It is a real recognition of the fact that evil is a parasite, not an original thing. The powers which enable evil to carry on are powers given it by goodness."

That is why, by the way, you see in J. R. R. Tolkien's *Lord of the Rings* that evil is clearly presented as a parasite on the good. When the ring is offered—the ring of power, the one ring that binds all other rings—it is offered as a temptation, because all these rings could be used with good intention. When the character Galadriel is asked to take the ring and keep it safe, she realizes that its corrupting influence would make her very great but also very terrible. Her intention to use it for good would not protect her from its evil power and the ultimate destruction of her people. The idea here is that we can give up our good power to an evil thing and empower its corruption to spread.

Lewis was trying to persuade his audience that the world we experience now is a distortion of a good creation. The good world changed as the result of the fall of Adam. Lewis strongly refuted the concept of dualism—that the universe contains equal and opposing forces of good and evil—yet he acknowledged that the New Testament refers often to the existence of evil within the universe. Lewis explained that the earth is now "enemy-occupied territory. . . . Christianity is the story of how the rightful king has landed, you might say landed in disguise, and is calling us all to take part in a great campaign of sabotage." Although the planet has been invaded by evil, Christ's incarnation was the counterinvasion to reclaim his kingdom.

At this point, Lewis addressed the issue of our free will and God's decision not to create automatons. It wouldn't be much of a relationship if God would have programmed us as machines that chant, "I love you." God is interested in our free response, but the danger there, of course, is that we can also reject him, which is what caused the mess in the first place. Lewis contended, "The happiness which God designs for His higher creatures is the happiness of being freely, voluntarily united to Him and to each other in an ecstasy of love and delight compared with which the most rapturous love between a man and a woman on this earth is mere milk and water. And for that they must be free."

Ultimately, he was arguing that our true dignity arises from the freedom of our will. There is a choice that we must make, and we cannot *not* make a choice. Either we will be moving toward God or away from him. God cannot give us a happiness and a peace apart from himself—there is no such thing. When God reveals that he wishes to give us happiness and peace and joy, he is saying that he is the wellspring of those conditions. And if we try to find joy in other sources, we will become bitterly disappointed and empty in the end. Seeking God isn't just an appendage to our lives; God is the very source of our well-being. This is poignantly illustrated in John 6:66–69 when Jesus turned to his disciples and asked, "You do not want to go away also, do you?" Jesus asked this question at a time when many of the people had begun to fall away because of dissatisfaction with Jesus' message. Peter responded with a question and answer that we all should ponder: "Lord, to whom shall we go? You have words of eternal life." In that moment, Peter recognized that every decision of the will ultimately comes down to that dichotomy: we walk either toward or away from our Savior; and if we walk away, we have rejected life itself.

Lewis then moved on to a discussion of Christ's authenticity. There is a famous paragraph, perhaps the best known in the book, concerning a concept Lewis termed the "trilemma":

I'm trying here to prevent anyone saying the really foolish thing that people often say about Him: "I am ready to accept Jesus as a great moral teacher, but I don't accept His claim to be God." This is the one thing we must not say. A man who was merely a man and said the sort of things that Jesus said would not be a great moral teacher. He would either be a lunatic—on a level with the man who says he is a poached egg—or else he would be the Devil of Hell. You must make your choice. Either this man was, and is, the Son of God: or else a madman or something worse. You can shut Him up for a fool, you can spit at Him and kill Him as a demon; or you can fall at His feet and call Him Lord and God. But let us not come with any patronizing nonsense about His being a great human teacher. He has not left that open to us. He did not intend to.

Lewis was saying that Jesus was either a liar or a lunatic, or he was as he claimed—God. Lewis presented a version of this same trilemma argument beautifully in his children's book *The Lion, the Witch and the Wardrobe*. Disbelieving Lucy's story of having visited a magical land called Narnia, her siblings go to speak to their guardian, an elderly professor. They are concerned that she is either lying or losing her sanity. After listening to their concerns, the professor responds, "There are only three possibilities. Either your sister is telling lies, or she is mad, or she is telling the truth. You know she doesn't tell lies and it is obvious that she is not mad. For the moment then and unless any further evidence turns up, we must assume that she is telling the truth" ([New York: HarperCollins, 2000], 48). While many people attempt to argue that Jesus was some kind of guru and was teaching esoteric truth, Lewis refuted that possibility on the grounds of who Christ claimed to be. If we accept that the New Testament documents are legitimate, primary historical sources, then we are left with only the option Lewis outlined.

Having provided a case for Christ's authenticity, Lewis went on to discuss the issue of repentance. He said, "Fallen man is not simply an imperfect creature who needs improvement; he is a rebel who must lay down his arms. . . . Now repentance is no fun at all. It is something much harder than merely eating humble pie. It means unlearning all the self-conceit and self-will that we have been training ourselves into for thousands of years. It means killing part of yourself, undergoing a kind of death." Our sin and need for repentance necessitate that Christ be who he claimed to be. Lewis asked, "What did he come to do? Well, to teach, of course; but as soon as you look into the New Testament or any other Christian writing you will find they are constantly talking about something different—about His death and His coming to life again. It is obvious that Christians think the chief point of the story lies there. They think the main thing He came to earth to do was to suffer and be killed." Lewis went on to state, "The central Christian belief is that Christ's death has somehow put us right with God and given us a fresh start."

This initiates another problem, however. Lewis explained, "Only a bad person needs to repent: only a good person can repent perfectly. The worse you are the more you need it and the less you can do it. The only person who could do it perfectly would be a perfect person—and he would not need it. . . . But supposing God became a man—suppose our human nature which can suffer and die was amalgamated with God's nature in one person—then that person could help us. He could surrender His will, and suffer and die, because He was man; and He could do it perfectly because He was God." This is Lewis's explanation of Christ as the "perfect penitent" and the Christian concept of atonement.

In his discussion of the incarnation of Christ, Lewis explained that God took upon himself our pain and sin: "We cannot share God's dying unless God dies; and He cannot die except by being a man. That is the sense in which He pays our debt, and suffers for us what He Himself need not suffer at all."

Lewis then drew his practical conclusion to these first two books by asserting, "In Christ a new kind of man appeared [and offered a] new kind of life . . . the Christ life." He explored this concept in these terms: "But the Christian thinks any good he does comes from the Christ-life inside him. He does not think God will love us because we are good, but that God will make us good because He loves us." Lewis elaborated on this idea in his chapter titled "Divine Goodness" in *The Problem of Pain*. He explained that because God loves us, he desires our perfection:

> God does not exist for the sake of man. Man
> does not exist for his own sake. "Thou hast
> created all things and for thy pleasure they
> are and were created." We were made not
> primarily that we may love God (though we
> were made for that too) but that God may love
> us, that we may become objects in which the
> Divine love may rest 'well-pleased'. To ask that
> God's love should be content with us as we
> are is to ask that God should cease to be God:
> because He is what He is, His love must, in
> the nature of things, be impeded and repelled
> by certain stains in our present character, and
> because He already loves us He must labor to
> make us loveable. ([New York: HarperCollins,
> 2001], 40–41)

In other words, God will infuse us with his life, and he will
bring us to a point where it will be possible to manifest that
new kind of life.

Lewis then responded to the question of why God doesn't
intervene openly or directly in our world? Why doesn't he
come now? Why did it have to be two thousand years ago?
Lewis warned,

> I wonder whether people who ask God to
> interfere openly and directly in our world
> quite realize what it will be life when He does.
> When that happens, it is the end of the world.
> When the author walks on to the stage the play
> is over. God is going to invade, all right: but
> what is the good of saying you are on His side

then when you see the whole natural universe melting away like a dream and something else—something it never entered your head to conceive—comes crashing in; something so beautiful to some of us and so terrible to others that none of us will have any choice left? For this time it will be God without disguise; something so overwhelming that it will strike either irresistible love or irresistible horror into every creature. It will be too late then to choose your side. There is no use saying you choose to lie down when it has become impossible to stand up. That will not be the time for choosing: it will be the time when we discover which side we have really chosen, whether we realized it before or not. Now, today, this moment, is our chance to choose the right side. God is holding back to give us that chance. It will not last for ever. We must take it or leave it.

The apostle Peter addressed this same issue: "The Lord is not slow about His promise [to return], as some count slowness, but is patient toward you, not wishing for any to perish but for all to come to repentance" (2 Peter 3:9). The passage then continues on with the scenario of what will one day occur when the day of grace is over and judgment comes. Although God could obliterate all evil this very instant, he would simultaneously conclude the era of grace for his creatures. He is a patient God!

Lewis then moved on to develop a theme that we see in

a lot of his books. His argument is that we are eternal beings and are moving toward either glorification or damnation. What do we see when we look at human beings? There are some people who become more joyful and Christlike as they walk with the Lord as the years go by. There is a quality of life about them that we do not see in an immature person. But we can also see that the old phrase is true: there is no fool like an old fool. There are some people who grow more self-centered, angry, and bitter.

Each of us is creating a persona—one like a heavenly creature or a hellish one. To quote from Lewis's essay "The Weight of Glory," "It is a serious thing to live in a society of possible gods and goddesses, to remember that the dullest and most uninteresting person you can talk to may one day be a creature which, if you say it now, you would be strongly tempted to worship, or else a horror and a corruption such as you now meet, if at all, only in a nightmare. All day long we are, in some degree, helping each other to one or other of these destinations. . . . There are no *ordinary* people" (*The Weight of Glory: And Other Addresses* [New York: HarperCollins, 2001], 45–46). By our daily decisions we are shaping our general direction in life. We are choosing to move toward God or away from him, but never remaining neutral. Our movement is imperfect but sure. Lewis used a chessboard metaphor in *The Great Divorce* to clarify the seriousness of our daily choices. In his analogy, he compared the decisions within time to the plays within a chess game. All of the "moves" are ultimately leading the player toward victory or defeat, toward fellowship with God or eternal divorce and separation.

Christian Behavior

The emphasis in book 3 of *Mere Christianity* is Christian behavior. Here Lewis explored morality as consisting of three specific dimensions. The first one is the social dimension of morality, including fair play and harmony among individuals. The second is personal morality, which means integrity. The third dimension is moral purpose or the process of defining the purpose of human life—why we were created and where we are heading.

Lewis employed an analogy of a ship at sea to explain these categories of morality. Lewis asked three essential questions regarding the ship: (1) How can one keep the ship from sinking while at sea? (personal ethics/morality); (2) How can one keep from colliding with other ships while at sea? (social ethics/morality); (3) Why is the ship at sea in the first place? (teleology or foundational ethics/morality).

Lewis argued that we mostly think about the social dimension of morality, less about personal integrity, and even more rarely about the purpose of life. Considering that every individual will live forever, Lewis continued, "there are a good many things which would not be worth bothering about if I were going to live only to seventy years, but which I had better bother about very seriously if I am going to live for ever. Perhaps my bad temper or my jealousy are getting gradually worse—so gradually that the increase in seventy years will not be very noticeable. But it might be absolute hell in a million years." In fact, if Christianity is true, hell is precisely the correct term for what it would be. So, "if individuals live only seventy years, then a state, or a nation, or a civilization, which may last for a thousand years, is more important than an individual. But if Christianity is true, then the individual is not only more important but incomparably more important, for he is everlasting and the life of a state or a civilization, compared with his, is only a moment." Therefore, we cannot ignore the personal dimension without doing that to our peril. God did not give us awareness of moral law merely so that we could live in harmony with ourselves and others. He gave moral law so that we could recognize our need for relationship with God—our created purpose.

Four Cardinal Virtues

In dealing with the area of personal ethics, Lewis discussed four cardinal virtues. He was looking at morality not only in terms of social relationships but also in terms of an individual's life. He focused on four cardinal ("hinge") virtues: prudence, temperance, justice, and fortitude. Lewis clearly understood that God's cardinal virtues or precepts were given to keep us safe and promote our well-being; but when we regard them in a legalistic way, they tend to become an end in themselves. If we grasp that they are meant to keep us from harm and lead us to God, they serve their rightful purpose. Lewis noted, "We might think that, provided you did the right thing, it did not matter how or why you did it—whether you did it willingly or unwillingly, sulkily or cheerfully, through fear of public opinion or for its own sake. But the truth is that right actions done for the wrong reason do not help to build the internal quality or character called a 'virtue,' and it is this quality or character that really matters."

Writer and playwright T. S. Eliot emphasized this same concept in his play about the martyrdom of Archbishop Thomas Becket, *Murder in the Cathedral*. Shortly before his murder, Becket faces the last of four tempters, one who urges him to seek martyrdom for the sake of power and deification. Becket responds, "The last temptation is the greatest treason: To do the right deed for the wrong reason" ([Orlando: Harcourt Brace & Company, 1964], 44). This is the significance and difficulty of the cardinal virtues. God desires that they draw us to him, but like the Pharisees, we often take more pride in our adherence to them.

In discussing these qualities, Lewis explained, "Prudence means practical common sense, taking the trouble to think out what you are doing and what is likely to come of it. . . . [God] wants a child's heart, but a grown-up's head. He wants us to be simple, single-minded, affectionate, and teachable, as good children are; but He also wants every bit of intelligence we have to be alert at its job." Lewis added that "anyone who is honestly trying to be a Christian will soon find his intelligence being sharpened." This assertion aligns well with 1 Corinthians 2:12–13, which states, "Now we have received, not the spirit of the world, but the Spirit who is from God, so that we may know the things freely given to us by God, which things we also speak, not in words taught by human wisdom, but in those taught by the Spirit."

What do we usually associate with temperance? Alcohol, generally. Lewis, however, suggests that the connotations of this word go much deeper than mere abstinence from the consumption of alcoholic beverages: "Temperance referred not specially to drink, but to all pleasures; and it meant not abstaining, but going the right length and no further." He continued, "One great piece of mischief has been done by the modern restriction of the word Temperance to the question of drink." Here Lewis broadened the definition: "It helps people to forget that you can be just as intemperate about lots of other things. A man who makes his golf or his motor-bicycle the center of his life, or a woman who devotes all her thoughts to clothes or bridge or her dog, is being just as 'intemperate' as someone who gets drunk every evening. Of course, it does not show on the outside so easily: bridge-mania or golf-mania do not make you fall down in the middle of the road. But God is not deceived by externals."

Lewis emphasized that the virtue of temperance focused on enjoying God's good gifts within God-given limits. He offered a picture of what temperance looks like in his novel *Perelandra*. Ransom, the protagonist, is a newly arrived visitor on another planet, and as he explores, he sees "globes of yellow fruit" hanging from the trees. After tasting it, he states that its flavor was beyond human description: "For one draught of this on earth wars would be fought and nations betrayed." Then he says that when he was about to pick and eat another, "it came into his head that he was now neither hungry nor thirsty. And yet to repeat a pleasure so intense and almost so spiritual seemed an obvious thing to do. His reason, or what we commonly take to be reason . . . was all in favor of tasting this miracle again. . . . But for whatever cause, it appeared to him better not to taste again. Perhaps the experience had been so complete that repetition would be a vulgarity—like asking to hear the same symphony twice in a day" ([New York: Scribner, 1996], 37–38). This passage depicts temperance for what it really is—not ascetic denial but proper enjoyment of God's good gifts.

Concerning justice, Lewis addressed the topic only briefly but stated that it involved more than just what goes on in the legal system. Justice encompasses fairness, honesty, truthfulness, and promise keeping. Our sense of justice reflects our understanding that God is righteous and just.

Fortitude, the fourth of the cardinal virtues, "includes both kinds of courage—the kind that faces danger as well as the kind that 'sticks it' under pain. 'Guts' is perhaps the nearest modern English." Lewis added that a person cannot practice any of the other virtues very long without needing this one.

So, in this section, Lewis explained how the Christian's character is forged by his or her choosing to live out these central virtues. I have noticed that our culture has shifted in dialogue from *virtues* to *values*. This change is a significant one. Virtues are embedded in a system of absolutes, while values are relative, contextualized, and no longer connected to an absolute structure.

As he transitioned into a brief discussion of social morality, Lewis introduced the issue of stewardship, or giving. He stated, "I do not believe one can settle how much we ought to give. I am afraid the only safe rule is to give more than we can spare." He further admonished his audience, "If our expenditure on comforts, luxuries, amusements, etc., is up to the standard common among those with the same income as our own, we are probably giving away too little. If our charities do not at all pinch or hamper us, I should say they are too small. There ought to be things we should like to do and cannot do because our charities expenditure excludes them."

He suggested that the reason we often don't give more is our fear of insecurity. All of us struggle with this sort of thing. His basic line on it is this: "I cannot learn to love my neighbor as myself till I learn to love God; and I cannot learn to love God except by learning to obey Him." He developed the theme that obedience results from trust.

In a little section on morality and psychoanalysis, Lewis observed, "God doesn't judge [man] on the raw material at all, but on what he has done with it." Some of us are psychically more adjusted than others. Some people have better internal material that they can build with, and some are just less neurotic. He tells us that it is not an issue of our actions; it is an issue of what we do with what we have been given.

So, there are some good people who should have been

great people, and there are mediocre people who may actually be more virtuous than good people, in one sense, because of where they started. God does not judge by external appearances but by the internal attitude of the heart. That is why comparisons among people can be systematically dangerous. External appearances can be deceptive. Lewis explained, "Every time you make a choice you are turning the central part of you, the part of you that chooses, into something a little different from what it was before. And taking your life as a whole, with all your innumerable choices . . . you are slowly turning this central thing either into a heavenly creature or into a hellish creature; either into a creature that is in harmony with God . . . or else into one that is in a state of war and hatred with God."

If we go back to the idea of morality, these are the three elements: Are you in harmony with God (moral purpose), with yourself (personal morality), and with others (social morality)? His argument is that we cannot be in harmony with others, or with ourselves, until we are in harmony with God. So, all three of these dimensions of morality connect into a cohesive whole. Therefore, if we truncate the process and just focus on social morality, we have no access to the source of power (God) to attain the virtuous life that Lewis was talking about.

Next Lewis drew a distinction between the sins of the spirit and the sins of the flesh, speaking of the animal self and the diabolical self. He argued, "The Diabolical self is the worse of the two. This is why a cold, self-righteous prig who goes regularly to church may be far nearer hell than a prostitute" (book 3, p. 95). I find myself making a marvelous distinction between the sin and sinner, and I do that with myself. Even though often I don't like myself, I still draw the distinction between my sin and myself. When I do something wrong, I may think, *That's really not me*. But when someone else does the same wrong thing, I cannot disconnect the two. Concerning this issue, Lewis suggested that we should show charity to ourselves and are called to show that same charity to others. "What really matters is those little marks . . . on the central inside part of the soul which are going to turn it, in the long run, into a heavenly or a hellish creature."

He also spoke of the great sin of pride as being the worst sin of all: "There is no fault which makes a man more unpopular, and no fault which we are more unconscious of in ourselves. And the more we have it in ourselves, the more we dislike it others . . . Pride is *essentially* competitive—is competitive by its very nature. Pride gets no pleasure out of having something, only out of having more of it than the next man. We say that people are proud of being rich, or clever, or good-looking, but they are not. They are proud of being richer, or cleverer, or better-looking than others." But, he noted, "In God you come against something that is in every respect immeasurably superior to yourself. Unless you know God as that—and therefore know yourself as nothing in comparison—you do not know God at all. As long as you are proud you cannot know God."

Three Theological Virtues

Lewis moved on from the cardinal virtues to discuss three theological virtues: charity, hope, and faith. Charity is more than an emotional feeling; it is a choice of the will to love. He made these key statements: "Do not waste time bothering whether you 'love' your neighbor; act as if you did. As soon as we do this we find one of the great secrets. When you are behaving as if you loved someone, you will presently come to love him." He reminded his readers, "Good and evil both increase at compound interest. That is why the little decisions you and I make each day are of such infinite importance . . . An apparently trivial indulgence in lust or anger today is the loss of a ridge or a railway line or bridgehead from which the enemy may launch an attack otherwise impossible." So, he proposed, "act as if you did" love a person. "Do not sit trying to manufacture feelings. Ask yourself, 'If I were sure that I loved God, what would I do?" When you have found the answer, go and do it." He referred to this as being an "affair of the will."

Then he proceeded to the virtue of hope. For Lewis, hope was not vague or evanescent but very rational. As Christians, we have hope because we know whom we have believed in. We have hope because God has provided us with glimpses of what to expect in eternity. The hope God gives is concrete; it is rooted in him and his character as revealed in Scripture. We must relate hope to a deep and profound longing all of us have that is not satisfied in this world. We have a longing that goes beyond our grasp. Lewis made this argument: "If I find in myself a desire which no experience in this world can satisfy, the most probable explanation is that I was made for another world."

Let those longings in your deep heart of hearts, which cannot be satisfied by any person or position or possession, evoke a truth that you are homesick and that you seek a country that you have not yet seen. You are waiting for that; and there are hints of home and realizations that you are not home yet, that you are a stranger and an alien, and that God is preparing you for an existence that is beyond your comprehension.

Lewis continued on to talk about faith, defining it as "the art of holding on to things your reason has once accepted, in spite of your changing moods." He did not draw a distinction between faith and reason. He was asserting that real faith clings to truth despite the fact that moods and circumstances vacillate. I am fond of this truth: *Either I can judge my circumstances in light of God's character, or I can judge God's character in light of my circumstances.*

This is beautifully illustrated in John the Baptist's question of Jesus, recorded in Matthew 11. John was in prison, awaiting execution, and he sent a message to Jesus, asking him, "Are You the Expected One, or shall we look for someone else?" (v. 3). This seems almost incomprehensible coming from John, Jesus' cousin and the final messianic prophet. He had baptized Jesus, heard the voice from heaven, and seen the dove descend. Now, his circumstance made him doubt the character of Christ. Yet Christ responded so tenderly and mercifully: "Go and report to John what you hear and see: the blind receive sight and the lame walk, the lepers are cleansed and the deaf hear, the dead are raised up, and the poor have the gospel preached to them. And blessed is he who does not take offense at Me" (vv. 4–6). Christ succinctly reminded John that faith is about him, not circumstance. John was reminded of the changeless, eternal, and sovereign nature of God, and he was assured that God can raise the dead. Faith had very little to do with John's feelings; it had everything to do with One in whom John's faith was placed. Faith has to do with clinging to God, and this faith must be fed. Ultimately, these three virtues—charity, hope, and faith—come only from God.

Beyond Personality

We now move on to the last book, which is *Beyond Personality*, or *The First Steps in the Doctrine of the Trinity*. Here Lewis considered the difference in the terms "making" and "begetting." In referring to Christ, the Scripture does not say that Christ was *made* but rather *begotten* (John 3:16; Hebrews 5:5 KJV). This is a very important distinction, because to *beget* means to produce out of one's own essence. Humans beget humans, and God begets God. The biblical concept of Christ is that there was never a time when Christ did not exist.

In contrast, to make or construct something refers to creating out of a different material. A bird makes a nest, a beaver builds a dam, and a human makes a computer. Lewis was stressing the point that what God begets is God and what a human begets is human. Between God and us there is a Creator-created distinction. However, this distinction does not exist between God and Christ. Lewis also established that believers in Christ are spiritually begotten of God (1 John 5:1; 1 Peter 1:3 KJV).

Lewis also contrasted two Greek terms for life: *bios*, meaning biological life, and *zoë*, which Lewis defined as spiritual life: "The spiritual life which is in God from all eternity, and which made the whole universe, is *Zoe. Bios* has, to be sure, a certain shadowy or symbolic resemblance to *Zoe*: but only the sort of resemblance there is between a photo and a place, or a statue and a man." Lewis talked about Christianity as a great "sculptor's shop. We are the statues and there is a rumor going round the shop that some of us are some day going to come to life." In this analogy Lewis promoted the idea that we can have a new kind of life in God, and that is what God is offering. We do not have this "Zoë" until it is infused in us. God is offering us his very life in this process.

Having spoken of this idea, Lewis moved on to discuss time and God's relationship with it. Because he is eternal, God transcends time and exists as the ever-present-tense "I Am." As you may well know, there is a lot of debate these days about the views of time. I would lean toward Lewis's concept that God exists outside the boundaries of time, for time was created by God for humanity, not for him. As with all aspects of his creation, God is never constrained by something of his own making. The concept of time also relates to the mystery of free will—the mystery of divine sovereignty and human responsibility. Here Lewis offered a hypothetical explanation of this mystery. He suggested,

> But suppose God is outside and above the Time-line. In that case, what we call 'tomorrow' is visible to Him in just the same way as what we call 'today'. All days are 'Now' for Him. He does not remember you doing things yesterday; He simply sees you doing them, because, though you have lost yesterday, He has not. He does not 'foresee' you doing things tomorrow; He simply sees you doing them: because, though tomorrow is not yet there for you, it is for Him. You never supposed that your actions at this moment were any less free because God knows what you are doing. Well, He knows your tomorrow's actions in just the same way—because He is already in tomorrow and can simply watch you."

At this point, Lewis returned again to the subject of the Trinity. He explained that Christ, who is the self-expression of the Father, invites himself into our lives, and we are being invited into the life of the Trinity. Trinitarian life is a kind of drama where there is movement and dance and delight, and believers in Christ are welcomed into the very heart of all things. Lewis's *Perelandra* brings this image to life in the description of the "Great Dance," which conveys something of what it is like to live in fellowship with God in glory. He describes all aspects of God's creation intertwining in light and harmony and fellowship. According to Lewis, "The words 'God is love' have no real meaning unless God contains at least two Persons. Love is something that one person has for another person. If God was a single person, then before the world was made, He was not love." The love of the Trinity was manifest in God's reconciliation of himself to fallen human beings. J. I. Packer examined this when he wrote about the Trinity's roles in the redemptive process. He explained that God the Father initiated the plan of salvation; that Christ the Son accomplished it through his incarnation, death on the cross, and resurrection; and that the Holy Spirit applies salvation to the believer's life through his indwelling and daily process of sanctification. Therefore, the Trinity is the source of all love, as well as the great demonstration of it.

The mystery of the Trinity makes Christianity unique. There are only three theistic religions: Judaism, Islam, and Christianity, and only Christianity talks of a love and intimacy in the Father-Son relationship and in a lover-beloved relationship. The idea of personhood finds its ultimate expression in the very nature of God. The Trinity is a mysterious, personal, and intimate community, and that is what we are being invited to. As Lewis wrote, "The Son of God became a man to enable men to become sons of God."

We are not little gods, but we are being called into the reception of God's very nature. Lewis symbolized this reception as the catching of what he called a "good infection." It is not something that we are trying to do or achieve, but something that we receive from God. Lewis explained that there will be imperfection in other carriers of Christianity. They will not be perfect in this world. He admonished, "But never, never pin your whole faith on any human being; not if he is the best and wisest in the whole world. There are lots of nice things you can do with sand, but do not try building a house on it."

The only one we can truly cast ourselves utterly upon is the living God and his unchanging character. He will then infuse his life in us, and this will spill over into our relationships with others. The life of God in us is a powerful new nature with the ability to make us people of good character and develop in these virtues, both cardinal and theological.

Is Christianity hard or easy? Lewis answered that in one sense it is easy and in another hard: "The almost impossible thing is to hand over your whole self—all your wishes and precautions—to Christ. But it is far easier to do than what we are all trying to do instead. For what we are trying to do is to remain what we call 'ourselves,' to keep personal happiness as our great aim in life, and yet at the same time be 'good'."

He was saying that the way we come to this new life is by dying to the other: "When He said, 'Be perfect,' He meant it. He meant that we must go in for the full treatment. It is hard; but the sort of compromise we are all hankering after is harder—in fact it is impossible. It may be hard for an egg to turn into a bird: it would be a jolly sight harder for it to learn to fly while remaining an egg. We are like eggs at present.

And you cannot go on indefinitely being just an ordinary, decent egg. We must be hatched or go bad." The hatching, I think, is our death and resurrection. Right now we are moving along in that hatching process.

Lewis then used a wonderful illustration about the problem he had with toothaches as a child. His mother would give him an aspirin, but he also knew she would take him to a dentist. He recalled, "I could not get what I wanted out of her without getting something more, which I did not want. I wanted immediate relief from pain: but I could not get it without having my teeth set permanently right. And I knew those dentists; I knew they started fiddling about with all sorts of other teeth which had not yet begun to ache. They would not let sleeping dogs lie, if you gave them an inch they took an ell."

That is what God is like. We may want to have enough of Christianity to get a little bit better in our marriages. He will perhaps do that, but it is not all we are going to get. Once we call him in, he is going to give us the full treatment. That is the problem. God is offering something far, far greater than what we ask for. God is easy to please but hard to satisfy. There is a profound description in Lewis's *The Great Divorce* that illustrates what God offers. Lewis depicted the rebirth of a man who had struggled with lust (personified by a pet lizard). Reluctantly, the man allowed an angel to kill the lizard, and as the protagonist observed, the man began immediately to grow strong and muscular, while the dead lizard resurrected into a beautiful stallion. Then nature sang out, "The Master says to our master, Come up. Share my rest and splendor till all natures that were your enemies become slaves to dance before you and backs for you to ride, and firmness for your feet to rest on. From beyond all place and time, out of the very Place, authority will be given you: the strengths that once opposed your will shall be obedient fire in your blood and heavenly thunder in your voice" ([New York: HarperCollins, 2001], 113). This is the very essence of what Christ calls us to as Christians. We, in our meager trust of his goodness, fear we will lose something in our submission and death to self. He, on the other hand, promises that for the first time in our existence we will be able to enjoy the very gifts we so fear losing. Lewis further clarified, "Imagine yourself as a living house . . . You thought you were going to be made into a decent little cottage. But presently he starts knocking the house about in a way that hurts abominably and does not seem to make sense . . . The explanation is that He is building quite a different house from the one you thought of . . . He is building a palace. He intends to come and live in it Himself." Lewis continued,

> The command *Be ye perfect* is not idealistic gas. Nor is it a command to do the impossible. He is going to make us into creatures that can obey that command. He said (in the Bible) that we were 'gods' and He is going to make good His words. If we let Him—for we can prevent Him, if we choose—He will make the feeblest and filthiest of us into a god or goddess, a

> dazzling, radiant, immortal creature, pulsating all through with such energy and joy and wisdom and love as we cannot now imagine, a bright stainless mirror which reflects back to God perfectly (though, of course, on a smaller scale) His own boundless power and delight and goodness. The process will be long and in parts very painful, but that is what we are in for. Nothing less. He meant what He said.

In the last chapter of the book, Lewis discussed the idea of being under new management and becoming new people—not improved people, but transformed people. He wrote, "People see (or at any rate think they see) men developing great brains and getting greater mastery over nature . . . I should not be surprised if, when the thing happened, very few people noticed that it was happening . . . It is not a change from brainy men to brainier men: it is a change that goes off in a totally different direction—a change from being creatures of God to being sons of God."

He concluded the book with a marvelous statement: "The more we get what we now call 'ourselves' out of the way and let Him take us over, the more truly ourselves we become . . . It is no good trying to 'be myself' without Him. The more I resist Him and try to live on my own, the more I become dominated by my own heredity and upbringing and surroundings and natural desires."

In other words, as we become more like Christ, we become more uniquely the persons we were meant to be.

We are not going to be defined by nature and environment, because we have within us the signal of transcendence. We cannot account for this transformation within our own nature. Again, C. S. Lewis developed this process in one of his other books, *The Voyage of the Dawn Treader*, one of the Narnia chronicles. In chapter 7, Eustace, a young boy, describes his own failed attempts to peel off his dragon scales (he had accidentally been magically changed from a boy into a horrible dragon). Every time he peeled off a layer of scales, another appeared just below it. Then a huge lion came up to him and offered to peel off the scales for him. Reluctantly, he allowed the lion permission, but the lion went much deeper than Eustace had been able to go. The process hurt tremendously, leaving Eustace a scale-free boy again but also very tender and sore. Then the lion cleansed and dressed Eustace's skin, completing the "un-dragoning" procedure. Lewis created an image for what Paul wrote in Colossians 3. We are able to "put on" the new self because our old nature has died and our new "life is hidden with Christ in God." There is something about this change that has the fragrance of God himself and that is Christ in us, the hope of glory.

Lewis explained that when we abandon the quest to try to become unique, we become unique. By losing our life in this world, we find it in Christ. When we give up ourselves, we will find our real selves. When we submit to the death of our ambitions and favorite wishes every day, submitting with every fiber of our being, we will find eternal life. We should keep back nothing. Nothing that we have not already given away will really be ours. Nothing in us that has not died will ever be raised from the dead. If we look for Christ, we will find him—and with him, everything else thrown in. Augustine once stated, "Love God and do as you please." Although this statement could be misapplied out of proper context, what he asserted is profound. If God is who we truly love, our desires will be holy and therefore appropriate. God does not ask us to forgo our passions. Instead, he calls us to passionately love him and know true passion and purpose in all of life.

Father, we thank you that you have a purpose for us, a glorious destiny, greater than that which we would have chosen for ourselves. Left to ourselves we would have sought only modest pleasures and ambitions. But you have something greater than that for us. It is your intention to make us fully conformed to the image of your Son. May we long for that, though we fear the process. May we trust you in what you take us through in order to bring about that utter satisfaction of becoming the people you intended us to be all along. We pray in Christ's name. Amen.

NOTES

NOTES

The Pilgrim's Progress

Introduction

John Bunyan's *The Pilgrim's Progress* holds a unique place in the history of English literature. It has touched a chord with readers for over four centuries, and it is one of the best-selling books of all time. It remains appreciated and beloved by many and has been translated into more than one hundred languages.

Bunyan lived in a turbulent time period known in English history as the Restoration. The regicide of Charles I took place in 1649, when Bunyan was only twenty-one years old. In the ensuing political upheaval, Oliver Cromwell, a Puritan military officer, established a temporary military rule termed "the Protectorate," which lasted from 1653 to 1658.

Cromwell's dictatorship was unpopular, for he introduced laws based on Puritan beliefs, the "blue laws," which prohibited swearing, singing, theater performances, and many social activities. Following this legalistic period, Charles II returned from a self-imposed exile in France, assumed the monarchy, and reinstated theater attendance and many previously prohibited activities. Cromwell's era of restraint was then followed by a period of rather unrestrained indulgence. Puritans were somewhat understandably unpopular, and during this social climate Bunyan lived, wrote, and preached. Partly as a result of his unpopular religious views and also for preaching without a license, he was arrested in 1660 and imprisoned for twelve years. It is believed that much of *The Pilgrim's Progress* was written during his imprisonment.

Although most people know Bunyan only for this famous allegory, he actually authored many works. He apparently had a pastor's heart and felt that certain heresies, as well as important biblical teachings, needed to be addressed in his own town of Bedford. The Quakers, under the inspiration of George Fox, were beginning to have an encroaching impact on Reformation theology. As a consequence, Bunyan aspired to communicate the doctrine of grace from a Calvinistic perspective and to write letters and other materials that communicated biblical truth. During the years of 1656–1657, Bunyan took part in written debates with some of the leaders of the Quaker movement. Bunyan authored such works as *Some Gospel Truths Opened*, *A Vindication of Some Gospel Truths Opened*, *A Few Sighs from Hell*, *The Doctrine of the Law*, and *Grace Unfolded*.

Although Bunyan was no stranger to writing, *The Pilgrim's Progress* was his first allegory. As he described it, the work took on a momentum of its own. In the prelude he explained, "When at the first I took my pen in hand thus for to write, I did not understand that I at all should make a little book in such a mode; nay, I had undertook to make another, which when almost done, before I was aware, I this begun." He went on to say, "And thus it was: I, writing of the way and race of saints in this our gospel day, fell suddenly into an allegory about their journey and the way to glory, in more than twenty things, which I set down; this done, I twenty more had in my crown, and they again began to multiply, like sparks that from the coals of fire do fly."

There is some debate over the date of the writing of *The Pilgrim's Progress*. Some claim that Bunyan did not write it in prison while others claim that he did. Many agree that he most likely began this work during the second half of his first imprisonment, probably between 1666 and 1672. He was released from prison for a brief period of time, and it may be that he actually completed the work around 1677 when he was finally set free. It is possible, of course, that he merely left it unpublished for a number of years. One thing is certain; he debated whether to publish it at all. He wrote, "Nor did I undertake thereby to please my neighbor: no, not I; I did it mine own self to gratify." His goal in writing the work, it seems, was more personal than public, but his decision to share it with others has blessed countless people over the centuries. In fact, the book became so popular that some years later he was prompted to write the second part of *The Pilgrim's Progress*. This work tells what became of Pilgrim's wife and children, who were left behind when Pilgrim went off on his journey toward the Celestial City.

Bunyan was born in 1628 and died in 1688. He wrote voluminously and, in fact, authored some sixty books—many of which were produced in prison. Most of Bunyan's imprisonment was spent simply writing or in ministering to fellow prisoners. He had only two books in his possession during his imprisonment: the Bible and Foxe's *Book of Martyrs*. Those who have read and appreciated *The Pilgrim's Progress* cannot deny Bunyan's dependence on Scripture in the development of his theme and characters. Charles Spurgeon, the great nineteenth-century London preacher, read *The Pilgrim's Progress* twice a year for over fifty years. This speaks to the spiritual depth that Spurgeon found in it. Spurgeon once said of Bunyan, "If you cut him he would bleed Bible."

The allegorical depth of Bunyan's work is almost impossible to grasp without a knowledge of Scripture, yet its general plot and purpose can be understood even by a young child. Bunyan filled his work with literally hundreds of allusions from all over the Scriptures—from Psalms to Isaiah to Revelation. Because of the generous incorporation of Scripture, *The Pilgrim's Progress* becomes a catechesis—a form of training in righteousness, faith, redemption, reconciliation, justification, and sanctification. This extraordinary book addresses such questions as how a person grows spiritually, the natures of heaven and hell, and the roles of angels, demons, and spiritual warfare in the lives of believers.

Many of the names used in this allegory, such as the Slough of Despond and Mr. Worldly Wiseman, are familiar to us because these terms have actually permeated our culture. Bunyan's book inspired other authors as well: William Thackeray's most popular novel, *Vanity Fair*, took its title from an image he remembered from *The Pilgrim's Progress*; Nathaniel Hawthorne appropriated Bunyan's allegorical structure for his tale *The Celestial Railroad*; William Blake painted a number of watercolors illustrating scenes from *The Pilgrim's Progress*; and C. S. Lewis was inspired by the allegorical imagery in this book. In fact, Lewis's first book as a Christian, *The Pilgrim's Regress*, is essentially in this style as he described his own journey from philosophical materialism to idealism, to pantheism, to theism, and finally to Christianity. Speaking of this journey in his third preface to *The Pilgrim's Regress*, Lewis wrote, "I thought that was fairly common procedure, that people went through those stages."

Allegory typically packs a powerful literary punch. While there is an obvious surface plot, there are additional layers of meaning that provide a provocative means of exploring truth. Allegory offers a compelling, indirect path to the truth when the familiar path has lost some of its appeal. Certain images used again and again have a way of losing their effect. That is one of the reasons C. S. Lewis's Chronicles of Narnia has been so effective in communicating the gospel story.

Bunyan used a dream framework as the structure for his allegory. The narration occurs within that context, and the observer awakes at the conclusion of the work, wishing that he or she, too, were a resident of the Celestial City. This format had been made very popular in the fourteenth century by Dante's *Divine Comedy*, and it is possible that Bunyan was influenced by that work. Like Dante, Bunyan developed characters who are used to personify virtues and vices. Through a series of dreams/visions, Bunyan's pilgrim journeys from the City of Destruction to the Celestial City, knowing in advance that there will be a price to pay for this pilgrimage.

Bunyan's Emphasis on Practical Theology

Bunyan's work emphasizes both the simplicity of the gospel and the costliness of grace. The main character in *The Pilgrim's Progress* is first introduced to the reader as "Graceless" but is renamed "Christian" after his burden of sin falls away at the cross. Bunyan's story recounts his awareness of sin, the impediments that hinder his journey to the cross (salvation), and the impediments and struggles he encounters along his walk through the world. The plot follows Christian through times of action as well as through periods of contemplation. He experiences trials, stresses, and failures, along with periods of refreshment and restoration. His journey parallels every believer's spiritual life. We, too, enjoy times of growth and action, but typically these result from times of testing, struggle, and reflection. As Christian illustrates, sometimes the journey is characterized by success and growth and at other times by discouragement, regression, failure, and despair. Along with Christian, the reader learns much about the friends and enemies of truth and the nature of Christian fellowship.

Bunyan employed rich descriptions, masterfully created characters, and numerous debates and dialogues, yet I believe Christian's fallibility to be one of the reasons why people relate so well to this story and its protagonist. He is an unlikely hero because of his many missteps. He falls prey to Wiseman, loses the parchment roll (the Scriptures), falls into the net of flattery, and leads another character astray through his vain confidence. This is not exactly what we would expect of a great hero. Yet that is part of the beauty of Bunyan's great story. Christian is the main character but not its hero; that role belongs exclusively to Christ, who saves both Christian's life and his soul. He is used to show that the most ordinary person is made extraordinary by pursuing God's purposes. So, the power of this story is its encouraging truth that we achieve not by our own power, but by Christ in us.

One reason why Christian is such a convincing character is that he is, in many ways, Bunyan himself. Bunyan's great autobiography, *Grace Abounding to the Chief of Sinners*, describes his own spiritual journey and stresses his personal encounter with Christ and his ensuing experiences. Its emphasis is not theoretical but practical. In the nitty-gritty details of day-by-day living, there exist dual worlds—the external experience of conflict inherent in the world's system and also the internal conflict of the soul with temptations. Bunyan was able to deeply layer his work because he struggled so intensely in the external and internal worlds.

Grace Abounding to the Chief of Sinners is not exactly bed-time material. It is, in some respects, an obvious chronicle of a melancholic, a person who went through fits of despair and depression and wondered if it were at all possible for him, the chief sinner, to lay hold of the grace of the living God. Bunyan personally experienced the "slough of despond," and he knew what it meant to be tempted by Mr. Worldly Wiseman.

There is a considerable emotional intensity in the stages of Christian experience depicted in *The Pilgrim's Progress.* The rich details and descriptions allow us to have a real sense of what Bunyan was seeking to express. He did not depend, as he clearly stated, on the opinions of other people. Bunyan was a man with very basic education, so his main stress was that a person's growth in the faith comes not by studying the philosophers but by digging deeply into the well of God's Word, drinking from that well, and being guided by the inspiration of the Holy Spirit.

So, when we see Christian and Faithful going into the house of Interpreter—as all pilgrims need to do—Interpreter represents the Holy Spirit, who illumines the Word of God to make it clear and fresh and applicable in our lives. I mentioned earlier that Bunyan had access to only two books while in prison: the Bible and John Foxe's *Book of Martyrs.* It is obvious that both texts shaped Bunyan's thoughts as he wrote.

For the Puritan, theology was, above all, practical.

They believed the Bible spoke to all issues and temptations of daily living. The Puritans were diligent students of Scripture, and when they gathered together, they would discuss God's Word and its application to their spiritual journeys. Similarly, in *The Pilgrim's Progress* we find that when two pilgrims meet, they discuss how each of them began the way of pilgrimage. They expound in great detail on these experiences and compare them. No two people in the story have identical experiences, which reminds us that God deals with individuals. While there are certain patterns that permeate the work, there are many variations because people are, in fact, very different.

I want to also note that this book is a realistic allegory, although this term may seem like an oxymoron, for there is powerful realism to this story. Regarding this, N. H. Keeble commented (in his preface to the 1984 Oxford World's Classics edition of *The Pilgrim's Progress*),

> Everything is visualized, in terms of the contemporary life that Bunyan knew. What we are dealing with, in all the kinds of encounters and the people and so forth, are really people that are seen, and their experiences are seen, in the circumstantial details of their journey, which takes us along a muddy, poorly sign-posted journey, over hills, through dark valleys and on 17th century roads, bleak moors exposed to inclement weather, sobered by the sight of criminal elements hanging from a wayside

divot, apprehensive of footpaths, fearful of being benighted and grateful for the refuge of an inn or house hospitable to strangers, sheer physical exhaustion, the weariness of aching legs, all these things and more are not far away.

We really get the idea of what it would have been like to live in East Anglia in the seventeenth century. Although the narrator ties the episodes of the story together, we do not depend on him very much for our information. Instead, the actual discourses of the characters provide the vast majority of the teaching and information.

We discover that Christian is constantly taxed to tell his friends from his foes, for those who appear to be friends often prove to be combatants in spiritual warfare. For instance, at the beginning of this work Christian becomes easy prey for Mr. Worldly Wiseman. Later, however, as he becomes more astute, he recognizes the fallacies of Mr. Money-love. He also insightfully identifies the weakness of a character called Littlefaith. As time goes on, he increases in discernment and spiritual alertness. Similarly, there is a need for all Christians to be sober and on the alert and avoid becoming a people who slide into complacency or who are seduced into sleep or torpor or inactivity.

Bunyan introduced characters such as Mr. Talkative and Ignorant in order to exemplify particular character flaws. As one person put it, Bunyan's characters are adjectival in nature; that is, they hint at attributes rather than essence, for people may be virtuous or vicious to a degree and yet not consumed by any single virtue or vice. This moral realism forms his artistic realism.

Bunyan used Evangelist, who represents the Word of God, to discern many weaknesses in Christian and Faithful. Through their interactions we see that faith coexists with failings—a comforting thought. There are characters, such as Littlefaith and Mr. Fearing, who finally make it to the Celestial City, yet not easily. Littlefaith and Mr. Fearing add to their trials by their lack of trust. Once again, Bunyan illustrated the important of perseverance. We see such characters as unlikely literary heroes, but they are people just like us, strengthened by the power of Christ.

Bunyan's point is that any man or any woman, through grace, can become a Christian hero. It is Christian's actual frailty and fallibility that arouse our sympathy for him. Bunyan concentrated in this book on God's gift of grace. While a robust Calvinistic view may debate the origin of the perseverance, Bunyan emphasized the practicality of perseverance in daily life.

Furthermore, the virtues that Bunyan's characters promote when they talk about the gospel are different from what we often hear today. Contemporary gospel messages typically focus on the love of God, the mercy of God, the compassion of God, and the embrace of God. What we rarely focus on is the holiness or judgment of God or the importance of fleeing from the wrath to come. These concepts are simply not welcomed. Yet I believe that dimension is a much-needed corrective for our culture because these attributes of God haven't changed. There is no new Bible that has eliminated these realities. Instead, what we have is a new culture that has eliminated discussion of unpleasant truths.

We are very adept at managing the biblical texts, focusing on the verses that we like and ignoring those that don't make us feel very good about ourselves. This is why we would prefer that Jesus had not said as much about hell as he did. Frankly, he spoke more about hell than anyone else in Scripture—he appeared rather serious about the topic. He also spoke about rewards more than anybody else, implying that the quality of our lives as pilgrims on this planet indeed have a bearing on the quality of our experience of eternity. I can't get around that. It doesn't go with the grain of our culture, but nevertheless it is there.

Old books often remind us of concepts our own culture has forgotten or overlooked. I think C. S. Lewis was right when he suggested that if we don't read "one for one [old books]," then we should at least make it "one for three." He meant that every time we read three new books, we should follow up by reading at least one old book (i.e., pre-Enlightenment). We need to read older books to gain perspective on the biases of our own time; otherwise, we risk becoming wholly enthralled by our cultural illusions. Modern people often fall prey to a dangerous presupposition that wisdom ends with us and our generation, that we know all things. It is not true.

Tone and Style

Bunyan's tone and style were very popular with his original audience. He did not believe, as did some preachers, in artistic sermons. Bunyan's approach was pitched to the practical mind. He lived in an agricultural community, and he didn't want to fill his sermons with metaphysical ingenuity. Rather, he spoke and wrote in an authentic, colloquial tone. When this book became so widely popular that he felt he needed to write a sequel, he resisted the temptation to elevate the style. The second part employs the same simplistic style, which led to considerable criticism. Critics claimed his work was that of a "'Grub Street hack,' so wanting in sublimity as to be quite unacceptable to men of quality." Those were the thoughts of the philosopher David Hume, for example. Others felt that to enjoy and esteem Bunyan was a sign of bad taste.

In many ways, *The Pilgrim's Progress* is the earliest English novel—or certainly a claimant for that—and it is our last allegory in this style, making it a bridge between the medieval world and the modern world. It reflects the paradoxical character of the pilgrim, whose religious tradition encouraged him not only to be a shrewd observer of people and their environments but also to detect great significance in what he saw.

We can see in this book a penetration of the visible by the invisible. The visible world points beyond itself to the invisible world. The things that we see and hear and taste and touch can be understood as intimations of a more profound, invisible world, and thus the allegorical style can take on genuine meaning. It is kind of a spiritualization of mortal experience.

For example, *The Pilgrim's Progress* reveals three common responses to the gospel through three different characters: Christian responds in faith, Obstinance rejects the message, and Pliable does whatever is convenient at the moment. Obstinance mocks the gospel messenger and lets him go, while Pliable, hearing his answers to Obstinance, is persuaded to go on the journey as well. Pliable journeys for a short time, but at the first difficulty he returns home. When the travelers encounter the Slough of Despond, Pliable is overwhelmed by the magnitude of the challenge. Later, when he abandons the journey, a character named Goodwill remarks, "Alas, poor man! is the celestial glory of so small esteem with him, that he counteth it not worth running the hazards of a few difficulties to obtain it?"

Bunyan's own life story, *Grace Abounding to the Chief of Sinners,* describes a man who understood this slough of despond very well. He wrote, "I thought now that every one had a better heart than I had; and could have changed heart with any body. I thought none but the Devil himself could equalize me for inward wickedness and pollution of Mind" (*Grace Abounding* [Boston: The Athenaeum Press, 1910], 84). This passage depicts a man under conviction for his sins and feeling the weight of despair. Bunyan continued,

> I fell, therefore, at the sight of my own vileness,
> deeply into despair; for I concluded that this

condition that I was in I could not stand with a state of Grace. Sure, thought I, I am forsaken of God; sure I am given up to the Devil, and to a reprobate mind. And thus I continued a long while, even some Years together. While I was thus afflicted with the fears of my own damnation, there were two things would make me wonder; the one was, when I saw old People hunting after the things of this life, as if they should live here always; the other was, when I found Professors much distressed and cast down, when they met with outward losses, as of Husband, Wife, or Child. *Lord, thought I, what ado is here about such little things as these! What seeking after carnal things by some, and what grief in others for the loss of them! If they so much labor after, and spend so many tears for the things of this present life, how am I to be bemoaned, pitied, and prayed for!* (*Grace Abounding*, 84–85)

Both Bunyan and Christian encountered sloughs of despond, and it is important to note that these metaphoric sloughs *preceded* salvation.

An Overview of Main Characters, Plot, and Symbolism

Bunyan's characters personify particular attributes. There are essentially only two categories of characterization in the book: godly characters and ungodly characters. Bunyan used these various people to portray both truth and spiritual dangers. Christian frequently struggles to distinguish his friends from his foes, for many are duplicitous. The godly acquaintances instruct, discipline, encourage, and fellowship with Christian, while the ungodly characters provide clear reminders of the spiritual warfare that we encounter daily as we make our pilgrimage through life.

Included in the godly group of characters is Evangelist, who leads Christian in his efforts to reach the Celestial City. In contrast, the ungodly Obstinate attempts to convince him to turn away from his destination, as do Worldly Wiseman, Atheist, Adam the First, and many others. Each of these negative characters represents an impediment or desire that distracts Christian from his goal, but as he encounters these individuals, he grows in both faith and knowledge. Each struggle and failure serves to strengthen him for future difficulties.

Mr. Worldly Wiseman, a resident of the town of Carnal Policy, represents religion pursued for the sake of secular advantage. He attends the "right" church, but he is indifferent to the message that is proclaimed. He merely wants to see and be seen because he seeks temporal position and praise. When Christian encounters Mr. Worldly Wiseman, he is initially influenced by him. However, Evangelist intervenes and rebukes him for being so easily dissuaded by the Slough of Despond and Mr. Worldly Wiseman. He admonishes Christian, saying, "See that ye refuse not him that speaketh. For if they escaped not who refused him that spake on earth, much more shall not we escape, if we turn away from him that speaketh from heaven." He goes on to remind Christian, "Now the just shall live by faith: but if any man draw back, my soul shall have no pleasure in him."

A short time later, Christian encounters Mr. Legality, who is also powerless to free him from his burden. Christian leaves the Way for a path that seems easier, but it leads him only to despair. Legality represents the law's inability to free anyone from bondage (Galatians 3). He is again encouraged by Evangelist to return to the Wicket Gate, which is the true entrance to the Way to the Celestial City. The Wicket Gate symbolizes the singular hope found in salvation through Jesus Christ, the narrow way of truth and life, spoken of in Scripture. Bunyan wrote, "Now, over the gate there was written, 'Knock, and it shall be opened unto you.' He [Christian] knocked, therefore, more than once or twice." This eager knocking intimates the desperate nature of his condition.

One other quote from Bunyan's own experience refers to a way of passage not unlike this Wicket Gate. He spoke about a wall: "About this wall I thought myself to go again and again, still prying as I went, to see if I could find some way or passage by which I might enter therein"; but he found himself blocked out from that way of life:

> But none could I find for some time. At the last, I saw, as it were, a narrow gap, like a little doorway, in the Wall, through which I attempted to pass; Now the passage being very straight and narrow, I made many efforts to get in, but all in Vain, even until I was well

nigh quite beat out, by striving to get in. At last, with great striving, methought I at first did get in my head, and after that, by a sidling striving, my Shoulders and whole Body. Then I was exceeding glad, and went and sat down in the midst of them, and was so comforted with the light and heat of their Sun. (*Grace Abounding*, p. 54)

After entering the Way, Christian comes to the house of Interpreter, who is a representation of the Holy Spirit. Here he is shown several rooms, each of which conveys a spiritual truth. First, he is taken into the parlor, an image of the human heart. The room is filled with dust, and although a servant sweeps it furiously, the dust merely fills the air and chokes the occupants. Then Interpreter commands that the room be sprinkled with water, a symbol of sanctification. Only after the water is sprinkled does the dust settle, making it possible to sweep the parlor clean. Interpreter explains, "He that began to sweep at first, is the Law; but she that brought water, and did sprinkle it, is the Gospel." Again, as emphasized in Galatians 3, the law is capable only of bringing us to awareness of sin; it is God's grace and sanctification that cleanse us of sin.

Here Bunyan provided a vivid contrast between law and grace. The law only stirs up that which is within us. Tell a person not to do something, and immediately he or she formulates all kinds of ideas about how to do it. There is a true story about a hotel in Houston that had a problem with people fishing from its second-floor balconies. Sometimes the sinkers on the fishing lines would be blown into the first-floor windows and crack them, to the great consternation of the hotel staff. Then the management decided to remove the "No Fishing from the Balcony" signs that were posted around the hotel, and the problem ceased. Ironically, it was the signs that gave the visitors the idea to fish from those hotel balconies. Similarly, while God's law delineates his standard and shows us what righteousness is, it cannot solve the sin problem. It can only reveal the problem. It is merely the tutor to lead us to Christ.

Next Christian encounters two children, Passion and Patience. Passion laughs at Patience for agreeing to wait a year for her good things; Passion wants everything immediately. These children represent those who choose their enjoyment in temporal pleasures during life versus those who defer their joy in favor of eternal contentment in heaven. (This principle is illustrated in Psalm 73.) Interpreter explains that, ultimately, "Patience will have to laugh at Passion, because he had his best things last; for first must give place to last, because last must have his time to come; but last gives place to nothing; for there is not another to succeed. He, therefore, that hath his portion first, must needs have a time to spend it; but he that hath his portion last, must have it lastingly." What Bunyan was highlighting here is the truth that those who pursue only temporal goods and pleasures enjoy them for a very short time, but those who pursue permanent things, heavenly treasures, enjoy them forever.

Then Christian is led to a place where a fire burns against a wall. Although a person continually throws water on the fire to put it out, it is not extinguished. Interpreter then takes Christian around to the back side of the wall and shows him another man who holds a container of oil. This man secretly fuels the fire with his oil, making it impossible for the person with the water to put it out. Interpreter explains, "This is Christ, who continually, with the oil of his grace, maintains the work already begun in the heart."

Finally, Interpreter guides Christian to the door of a palace, where he encounters heavily armed people. Here he discovers that he must put on the armor of God—the sword of the Spirit, the shield of faith, and so forth. He also meets a pilgrim imprisoned in an iron cage. This man represents one who at one time professed faith yet later rejected God in favor of pleasure and experiences. He explains that he has grieved the Holy Spirit and rejected God, so God has abandoned him. Bunyan implied that it is possible for a person to become so hardened against God and his Word that salvation is no longer possible.

After Christian leaves Interpreter's house, he encounters a cross on a hill. At this cross his burden finally falls away into a sepulcher. Then three Shining Ones come and salute Christian: "'Peace be to thee.' So the first said to him, 'Thy sins be forgiven.' The second stripped him of his rags, and clothed him with change of raiment. The third also set a mark on his forehead, and gave him a roll with a seal upon it, which he bid him look on as he ran.'" The first Shining One alludes to the Father, who tells him that his sins are forgiven. The second represents the Son, who strips him of his rags and gives him new clothes from his own righteousness. The third represents the Holy Spirit, who sets him apart with a mark and gives him the certificate—a roll with a seal—for the day of redemption; Christian is saved and set apart as a child of God.

It is not long after this time of relief and joy that Christian's new faith is assaulted in a variety of ways. He meets characters named Simple, Sloth, and Presumption. The first symbolizes ignorance, the second indifference and complacency, and the third arrogance and risk. Christian next meets a man named Formalist and another named Hypocrisy. These characters represent those who merely go through the motions of religiosity and pretend to be what they are not.

Next Christian discovers the Hill of Difficulty, and midway to the top of the hill, he finds a pleasant arbor. He decides to turn aside only for a short time but spends a good deal more time there than he planned. As a consequence, he falls into a deep sleep and misses some significant opportunities. When he awakes, self-satisfaction and complacency become dangerous temptations. As he continues up the hill, he realizes that not only is he quite late, but he has left his roll behind—the certificate he will need to enter into the Celestial City. So, he has to backtrack, and, as a consequence, he runs into more difficulties.

Later, there is an inquiry that takes place when Christian comes to a stately palace called Beautiful. This palace provides an image of the church. There is a porter's gate, and the porter's name is Watchful. Watchful tells him that the house was built for the Lord of the Hill and for the relief and security of pilgrims. Various people in this palace then catechize Christian. One of the instructors is named Discretion; he inquires into Christian's profession of faith before he is admitted into the palace, symbolizing that those who make profession of faith need to be examined before being accepted into the fellowship as members of the church.

Christian is also questioned by three others. One named Piety asks whether he has a real desire to do God's will. Prudence seeks to examine his heart, and it is here that Bunyan described the great struggle from within, between nature and grace, which is Paul's Romans 7 experience. Charity says to Christian, "Have you a family? Are you a married man?" She inquires about the disposition of his family members and whether he sought to bring them with him. When he passes this examination, he is brought into the fellowship of that group. They sit down to supper, symbolic of Communion, the Lord's Supper.

That night he stays in the Chamber of Peace. The next day he is shown records of great antiquity and given an understanding of God's work and methods throughout history. He is shown a panorama of God's remarkable works and is even given a vision of the Delectable Mountains—a foretaste of heaven.

As Christian journeys, he comes to two valleys: the Valley of Humiliation and the Valley of the Shadow of Death.

The Valley of Humiliation reminds the reader of the danger of pride and self-sufficiency, for it is often adversity and tribulation that humble us to receive God's grace and rely on his power rather than our own. It is in this valley that Christian encounters Apollyon, the destroyer. In this encounter Christian relies on the shield of faith until the sword of truth is knocked from his hand. He fears he is about to be destroyed, but by the grace of God he is able to reach out and grasp the sword again. It is this sword that enables him to defeat his adversary, symbolizing the power of God's Word to protect and strengthen us for battle. Ultimately, Christian humbles himself and exalts Christ in the process. The accuser is used by God in the process of humbling Christian.

Christian then travels to the Valley of the Shadow of Death, which symbolizes spiritual distress. It is a solitary place, and Christian is warned about a deep ditch on one side, which represents the false doctrine of false security, and a very narrow path between that and a dangerous crag on the other side, which speaks of the despair of mercy. These represent two extremes into which a believer can slip: one is the presumption of grace, and the other is the disbelief that grace is offered and available. At this point in his journey, Christian can depend only on prayer to help him; it is his only effective weapon in this lonely place.

While in the valley, Christian encounters a fiend who speaks blasphemously to him, and he even begins to believe the fiend's thoughts are his own. When he looks back at the valley the next morning, he realizes there is no way he could have made it through the darkness alone; there were all kinds of hobgoblins and demonic creatures to obstruct him. He then recognizes God's presence and his use of adversity to mature him. In life there are lessons that cannot be learned from books; we must discover our weaknesses and God's sufficiency in those dark valleys.

Faithful becomes a very significant character at this point in the story. Bunyan used the dialogue between Faithful and Christian to highlight a number of significant truths. As the men travel along, they encounter a variety of tempters, including Adam the First, a personification of the flesh. Adam is an old man with three daughters: the Lust of the Flesh, the Lust of the Eyes, and the Boastful Pride of Life. These characters illustrate the unwillingness of humans to submit to God. Adam the First provides a stark contrast to Adam the Second (Christ), who willingly submitted himself to death, even on a cross, conquering the flesh.

As they walk along, Faithful tells Christian about some of his struggles on the way to the Celestial City. He relates an encounter with Discontent. He explains that Discontent left him disdaining friends and feeling afraid to share the gospel. Faithful then realized his call to boldly affirm Christ and his gospel. Although Christian and Faithful have fought different battles, they are able to encourage and rebuke each other and thus provide companionship and accountability.

At one point in the story, Faithful and Christian engage in a lengthy conversation with a man named Talkative. Talkative uses many words, but his life is characterized by inactivity. He is a hearer of the Word but not a doer. Bunyan offered this description of their conversation: "And this truly resembleth Talkative; he cheweth the cud, he seeketh knowledge, he cheweth upon the Word, but he divideth not the hoof, he parteth not with the way of sinners; but as the hare he retaineth the foot of a dog, or bear, and therefore he is unclean." According to Old Testament law, a clean animal had to chew cud and have a divided hoof. Bunyan used this analogy to illustrate that while Talkative may know the Word, he does not understand or know its power. Eventually, Talkative goes his own way because he cannot endure the conviction he experiences as he talks with Christian and Faithful.

Christian and Faithful transition from internal to external conflict as they come to Vanity Fair. Here Evangelist appears for the third time and tells them that one of them will soon die and reach the Celestial City before the other. In Vanity Fair the humble travelers offend the citizens because their dress is different and they do not speak the language of the city. Instead, they speak the language of Canaan, a metaphor for the word of truth. As a consequence, they are arrested and brought before a judge and jury. The judge is named Lord Hate-good, and the jury is composed of Mr. Blindman, Mr. No-good, Mr. Malice, Mr. Love-lust, Mr. Live-loose, Mr. Heady, Mr. High-minded, Mr. Enmity, Mr. Lyar, Mr. Cruelty, Mr. Hate-light, and Mr. Implacable. This jury convicts Faithful, and he is executed in a vile and painful way. His martyrdom, however, inspires a city resident named Hopeful to become a pilgrim, and Hopeful joins Christian.

Together they encounter a variety of troublesome characters, including Mr. Hold-the-world, Mr. Money-love, and Mr. Save-all. Mr. Hold-the-world covets this world's goods, saying, "For my part I like that religion best that will stand with the security of God's good blessings unto us; for who can imagine that is ruled by his reason, since God has bestowed upon us the good things of this life, but that he would have us keep them for his sake." These three characters are all self-centered and seek only to secure earthly benefits for themselves.

Next the two encounter Demas, who calls to them to "turn aside hither, and I will show you a thing." Hopeful is tempted to go and see, but Christian warns, "I have heard of this place before now, and how many have there been slain; and besides, that treasure is a snare to those that seek it, for it hindereth them in their pilgrimage." The value of Christian's companionship is beautifully illustrated in this and other temptations they experience. Soon after the temptation by Demas, the men come to the pillar that is Lot's wife. Hopeful then says, "I am sorry that I was so foolish, and am made to wonder that I am not now as Lot's wife; for wherein was the difference 'twixt her sin and mine? She only looked back, and I had a desire to go and see." He affirms then that "the grace of God is deeply mysterious."

When they discover a pleasant river, the two companions enjoy a time of refreshment, but that leisure distracts them, and they lose the ardor of the journey. They are side-tracked into By-path Meadow, where Christian's presumption convinces them to go over the stile onto a way that appears easier. Yet this path leads them farther and farther away, prompting Christian to later reflect, "Then I thought that it is easier going out of the way, when we are in, than going in when we are out."

The path leads them to Doubting Castle and a giant named Despair, illustrating the problems that arise when we turn aside from Christ and place our trust in ourselves. The men are imprisoned in a dungeon, but at a point when all seems lost, they begin to pray. It is then that Christian remembers he possesses a key that will allow them to open the locks and return to the King's highway again. The key symbolizes the power of prayer in the life of the believer.

Once back on the true path, the pilgrims ascend into the Delectable Mountains, where they experience both trials and delights. Here they meet shepherds named Knowledge, Experience, Watchful, and Sincere, all of whom represent qualities found in a good pastor or minister. As a shepherd of the Lord's sheep, a pastor needs to have knowledge of the Word, personal experience, loving care for the flock, and sincerity. His desires and actions need to always be directed in the best interest of the flock. Similarly, these shepherds guide and instruct the two pilgrims and encourage them on their journey. But then the men encounter Ignorance, a traveler who did not come in by the Wicket Gate. Instead, Ignorance climbed over the wall into the Way and remains ignorant of grace. Because he has no roll to admit him to the

Celestial City, he is ultimately turned away when he arrives. He represents those who still refuse grace in favor of their own efforts, and his fate is a tragic reminder of our insufficiency apart from Christ's work on our behalf on the cross.

Finally, the pilgrims arrive in the country of Beulah, and the Shining Ones appear again. Christian and Hopeful become sick with desire for the heavenly city, alluding to an image from the Song of Solomon. The final barrier is a river, which represents death. When they fail to find a bridge over the water, they inquire whether there is any other way to get to the Gate. The answer comes, "Yes, but there hath not any, save two, to wit, Enoch and Elijah, been permitted to tread that path since the foundation of the world." It then becomes clear that the travelers must go into the river, a final test of their confidence in God. Part I concludes with Christian's reception into the Celestial City.

I will not take time to deeply explore Part II of the book, but it is the story of Christian's wife, Christiana, and her pilgrimage as she guides her four sons to the Celestial City. One of my favorite passages from this section of the book involves a pilgrim who is ushered into the Master's banquet table. As he goes in, he says, "I see myself now at the end of my journey; my toilsome days are ended. I am going now to see that head that was crowned with thorns and that face that was spit upon for me. I have formerly lived by hearsay and faith, but now I go where I shall live by sight and shall be with Him in whose company I delight myself." What a beautiful description of the homecoming to be enjoyed by every believer.

Application

If you were to appear as one of Bunyan's characters, what name might be most appropriate for you? It is an interesting question to ponder. Each of us is called to pilgrimage. We are called to grasp the truth that the world is filled with allurements that would distract us from Christ and the cross. Bunyan's work encourages us to press on, to live in confident faith in Christ's sufficiency, and to anticipate the day when we shall live by sight. It is also a poignant reminder of how much we need the church for instruction and encouragement. As Christian learns, the journey does not necessarily get easier as we grow older; the challenges merely change.

Yet Scripture reminds us of the glory of one day hearing God greet us with "Well done, good and faithful servant" (Matthew 25). I believe that our regret when we see the living God will be our inability to follow him with fidelity; the pain and adversity will vanish. Paul reminds us that life is much like a race; it demands our all and exhausts our energy. Yet if we run the race to completion, we will receive the prize at the end. Oh, that we might live life as an echo of Paul's words in 1 Corinthians 9:24–26: "Run in such a way that you may win. . . . They then do it to receive a perishable wreath, but we an imperishable. Therefore I run in such a way, as not without aim."

Father, we thank you for this opportunity to reflect on these marvelous images. I pray that you would cause us to embrace the mindset that we seek a country and city whose architect and builder is God. Help us to recognize that no earthbound joy or felicity could ever satisfy our deepest longings. Cause us to grow in longing for what you have for us, and cause us to be a people who understand that in this world, we face tribulation. Help us to take courage because the Lord Jesus has overcome the world, and we are overcomers in him. In his name we pray. Amen.

NOTES

NOTES

The Brothers Karamazov

Introduction

No other novelist explored the souls of his characters so completely as did the Russian author Fyodor Dostoyevsky (1821–1881). I believe *The Brothers Karamazov* is his finest achievement, although he may be better known for *Crime and Punishment*. *The Brothers Karamazov* was completed in the last two years of his life. Dostoyevsky, however, did not regard the novel as complete, and he had planned to conclude some of the novel's unfinished themes. In a letter to his publisher upon its initial submission, he anticipated living another twenty years, but he died within two months of making that statement. Yet, as it stands, *The Brothers Karamazov* is a remarkable work that explores the whole human range of behavior, from the depths of depravity to the heights of exultation and from the meanness of the human spirit to the great nobility of which it is capable.

The Brothers Karamazov is a grave and absorbing literary accomplishment, and yet I believe that it is often misunderstood. Many literary critics refuse to take the novel on its own terms. Instead, they impose external ideas and assert that it is too didactic, misinterpret it as being Slavophilic, or deem it too politically conservative, accusing the author of trying to nostalgically reconstruct a past that never existed. I believe these criticisms to be faulty because they fail to accept the novel for what it is. They fail to appreciate Dostoyevsky's own vision of the novel, a vision clearly outlined in many of his letters. The honest reader can actually discover the author's purpose.

One of the fundamental errors some have made when analyzing this novel is to extract the story of the Grand Inquisitor from its context and regard his accusations as the central theme. The account of the Grand Inquisitor is, more accurately, the great argument against God's existence and love, which the rest of the novel rebuts. The chapter that introduces the Grand Inquisitor is followed by one about the elder, Zosima, and the Christian vision of sacrificial love and suffering that can lead to redemption. The author promoted the Christian view of redemption through the experiences of his characters, particularly three central characters—the Karamazov brothers.

The novel's literary structure is extraordinarily subtle because it is indirect. In his refutation of the arguments Ivan raises in the story of the Grand Inquisitor, Dostoyevsky used a plurality of voices—by means of an omniscient, third-person narration—to deny the scandalous claims against God. In doing so, Dostoyevsky detached himself from his characters. The reader is forced to interact with the plot without preconceptions and to question where all these discordant voices are moving as they go about their journeys. The book introduces significant theological and political issues relevant to readers of all time periods.

Dostoyevsky's Transformation

Dostoyevsky's life and writings were transformed by his imprisonment and exile. As a young man, he became a member of the Petroshevsky Circle, a revolutionary group that plotted against the czarist regime. As a result of his association with this subversive group, he was arrested and brought to trial. He was sentenced to be executed on December 22, 1849; however, as he and his coconspirators stood before a firing squad, their sentences were unexpectedly commuted to Siberian exile by the czar. During four years of exile, followed by another four years during which he was forbidden to return to Moscow, he diligently read the New Testament. As he reflected on the futility of the kind of idealism that he had formerly embraced, he gradually moved away from rational humanism and political idealism—that all human problems can be solved politically—and returned from exile with a religious mission.

After this experience all of Dostoyevsky's novels demonstrate the decisive change he experienced, politically and spiritually. His writings promote the theme that moral transformation can be brought about only by an encounter with Christ and an understanding of love and sacrificial suffering. After his return from prison, Dostoyevsky wrote *The House of the Dead*, which refers to his experiences in prison. He then wrote *Notes from the Underground* in 1864, the story of a man who is a type of existentialist hero—a person who seeks to preserve moral and personal choice in the face of threats imposed by reason, contingency, and self-interest. In this hero, Dostoyevsky's intention was to demonstrate humanity's need for Christ. His publication censor, however, eliminated that particular part of the story. In a letter to his brother in March 1864, Dostoyevsky wrote, "That swine of a censor. The passages where I jeered at everything and sometimes blasphemed *for form's sake* he let through, but he suppressed the place from where all this I deduced the need for faith and Christ" (William J. Leatherbarrow, *The Brothers Karamazov* [Cambridge: Cambridge University Press, 1992], 8). Because of the unintended censorship, this work does not represent Dostoyevsky's views as accurately as some of his other works.

Crime and Punishment followed in 1866 and is a masterwork novel. Its protagonist, Raskolnikov, theorizes that he can prove the nonexistence of God, and therefore of absolute law, if he can murder with impunity. He speculates that guilt is merely a social construct that impedes the exceptional man. Yet before and after his murderous experiment, Raskolnikov is plagued by irrational thoughts and guilt. While he had believed that reason alone could guide him, he finds himself incapable of reason once he has committed his crime. He also discovers that his breach of law has alienated him not only from others but also from himself. Ultimately, his intolerable loneliness and pain lead him on a path to Christ and salvation. In both *Crime and Punishment* and another novel, *The Idiot*, the author employed Christlike characters who reveal love to those who struggle. Sonya represents Christ to Raskolnikov through her sacrificial love as she empties herself out for others, while *The Idiot* develops the character of a prince, Myshkin, who is a Christlike figure at odds with his culture and the world. He is adrift in a setting where his trust in love, beauty, and compassion is completely out of place. In both of these novels, Dostoyevsky portrayed love, not power, as the vital force by which lives are changed and redeemed.

All Dostoyevsky's novels are characterized by these themes. His body of work also examines the conflict between ancient and modern Russia resulting from Peter the Great's aggressive efforts to reeducate and Westernize Russian intellectuals and society. Dostoyevsky believed that the individualism of Western society and its secularized notion of human nature led to loss of communal identity, one's sense of a moral compass, and disintegration of the social guidelines embraced by Christian orthodoxy. He feared for the implications of a shift toward Western ideals and philosophy and warned of the dangers in his various works.

In *The Gambler*, as well as in *The Devils*, also called *The Possessed*, Dostoyevsky further developed the conflict between personal freedom and moral responsibility. *The Brothers Karamazov* was written in the last years of his life, and in this novel he succeeded in creating a convincing Christlike figure in Father Zosima, in whom the healing power of love and the earthiness of his humanity reveal a glimpse of the incarnate Christ—the God-man. Generally, it is easier for an author to create vicious figures; to create one who is positive and not preachy, both credible and Christlike, is a great literary achievement. Father Zosima is the author's answer to the basic objections against the existence and love of the living God.

The Plot

The Brothers Karamazov develops a fairly simple plot, although in its extraordinary, subtle interconnections it resembles a great cathedral. While a cathedral is built in the simple shape of a cross, it incorporates many interesting features, such as flying buttresses, the nave, chapels, and the chancel; and so it is with this novel, as well. The main plot has to do with murder and money, yet a complex network of subplots helps to illuminate its theme. The murder is patricide—the death of a father—Fyodor Pavlovich Karamazov. He is a corrupt and lascivious provincial landowner and the father of three sons. The novel is structured around these sons. The first is named Dmitri, and he is a sensual man indeed. Dmitri is the son of Karamazov's first wife. After her death, Fyodor then has two more sons by a second wife: Ivan, a brilliant and intellectual skeptic, and Alyosha, a novice monk under the tutelage of the local monastic elder, Father Zosima. The novel also introduces another character named Smerdyakov, who is suspected of being Fyodor's illegitimate son by a local girl who is mentally disabled. Smerdyakov works as a servant in the Karamazov household and represents a distorted image of the character of the three legitimate sons.

Fyodor Karamazov lives a life of abject sensualism, indulging his appetite for experience in depraved ways. His eldest son follows in his father's footsteps, also living a life of selfish debauchery. The second son, Ivan, rejects sensuality for rationality. He argues that reason alone governs human actions and rejects the existence of any divinity, asserting that the human will is supreme. Alyosha embraces traditional Christian orthodoxy and serves as a bridge between his father and brothers. He attempts to unite his family and bestows both love and forgiveness liberally.

When Fyodor Karamazov is found murdered, suspicion immediately falls on Dmitri for several reasons. Dmitri's passionate nature, problems with money, and resentment over having been abandoned and cheated out of his inheritance make him a prime suspect. Furthermore, Fyodor and Dmitri have been engaged in a sexual rivalry over a local seductress by the name of Grushenka. Her charms have already enticed Dmitri away from Katerina, the woman to whom he is betrothed.

All these potential motives circumstantially indicate the guilt of Dmitri, and so he is brought to trial for the murder. He is ultimately found guilty and sentenced to imprisonment in Siberia despite the fact that it is discovered that Smerdyakov, not Dmitri, killed Fyodor. Although it is Smerdyakov who actually murdered Fyodor, as the story develops it is obvious that the three brothers also bear some responsibility for their father's death. Dmitri, through his example, encourages Smerdyakov to abandon moral restraint, but it is Ivan's ideological arguments that prove most convincing to the impressionable man. Some time after Fyodor Karamazov's murder, Smerdyakov confronts Ivan: "I did have a thought previously, sir, that with that kind of money I could begin a new life, in Moscow or even abroad, that was the dream I had, sir, all the more so because I thought that 'all things are lawful.'" Here he is quoting from Ivan's previous discourse. He continues, "It was true what you taught me, sir, for you told me a lot about that then: for if there is no infinite God, then there is no virtue, either, and there is no need of it whatever. That was true, what you said. And that was how I thought, too." The atheistic Ivan promotes a view of the will as supreme, arguing that in the absence of anything divine, good and evil do not exist. Smerdyakov is greatly influenced by Ivan's assertion that if God does not exist, then all things are permissible. Finally, Alyosha's passivity and naiveté further contribute to the murder. Yet through each brother's awareness of his own culpability, Dostoyevsky solidifies his theme.

At the novel's conclusion, Dostoyevsky's redemptive purpose is most evident. Katerina chooses to remain and look after Ivan, who has suffered a mental breakdown following his realization of the part he played in his father's murder. Ivan grasps that it was his faulty ideology that led to the crime, and his conscience leads him to confess to the crime during the trial. Yet when there is no corroborating evidence and after Smerdyakov has committed suicide, Dmitri is still convicted. Grushenka, however, reforms as the result of an encounter with Alyosha and decides to accompany Dmitri into exile in Siberia, where suffering proves powerfully instructive to him. The novel ends with Alyosha leaving the refuge of the monastery to go out into the world and live and serve as a Christian monk.

Style

The architecture of this extraordinary novel follows a law of balance, symmetry, and proportionality. It is beautifully constructed and ideologically complete. From the notes that Dostoyevsky left behind, it is obvious that the work was carefully crafted and combines artistic myth with religious mystery. It provides powerful images that illustrate that the human heart is the battlefield between the forces of good and evil; the locus of spiritual warfare is in the human soul. Each brother comes to grips with his own fallen nature and discovers the path to redemption. The novel presents confrontations between order and disorder, harmony and chaos, justice and injustice, and unity and fragmentation of both relationships and minds. Its artistic form probes the psychological, social, moral, and metaphysical dimensions of life.

One modern theme that makes this novel resonate with current culture is that of alienation. I am convinced that *The Brothers Karamazov* has influenced the development of the twentieth-century novel more than any other, principally because of this theme of alienation. Alienation is presented as a result of the loss of spiritual certainty, faith, and the power of reason, all of which sustained people in previous ages. The demise of human connectedness then becomes inevitable, for uncertainty, anxiety, and doubt about the human condition pervade life. This vacuum produces a longing for new certainties—a desire for clarity, moral certainty, and a significance that we cannot seem to find. Dostoyevsky's novels continue to speak powerfully to the human predicament, for they chronicle the schism created when human beings eradicate God from life and law.

There is a powerful antithetical structure employed in this novel, a contrast between moral monsters and characters who embody goodness. The monastery, a reminder of God's presence in his world, is juxtaposed with the town, Chermashnya, which means "cattle pen." Dostoyevsky seemingly uses this to establish a contrast between the biblical image of the shepherd protecting his sheep within the fold with the mere containment of cattle awaiting death (an existentialist view of life). There is a stark contrast between individual value of each sheep to the shepherd and the insignificance of the penned cattle. Apart from God, human beings are essentially reduced to the status of mere animal, existing without purpose or hope. There is also an important contrast between the Grand Inquisitor and the elder monk, Father Zosima. The Grand Inquisitor seeks to prove Christ's death a resounding defeat, while Father Zosima presents sacrificial love as the only means by which redemption is possible.

The antithetical parallels of the novel are further observed in Dostoyevsky's exploration of humanity's moral disintegration. Dostoyevsky viewed the fragmentation of the family as the symptom of a growing secular culture and held it largely responsible for the loss of a sense of moral continuity, community, and collective good in the world. On the one hand, *The Brothers Karamazov* is a memorial to what once was, and in another sense, it is prophetic and anticipates an ideal possible only within the kingdom of Christ. It also focuses on the dichotomy of human nature, as explored in his presentation of the fatal Karamazov nature. This nature is described in the courtroom scene in the following way: "[It was] capable of accommodating all kinds of opposites and of contemplating both abysses, the abyss above us, the abyss of the loftiest ideals, and the abyss below us, the abyss of the very lowest, stinking degradation." This conflicted nature illustrates the fragmentation of humanity that resulted from the fall. One part of us yearns for something higher, yet we feel a downward pull toward something lower. Here the novelist appears to be incorporating aspects of medieval philosophy, which holds that because of the fall, humanity exists in an incurable moral tension. We inherently recognize that we were created in the image of God and aspire to embody that image. Yet the fall has rendered our wills subservient to sin, and we perpetually succumb to animalistic instinct and sinful urges. There is a craving for harmony and an innate desire for beauty that cannot be achieved by human merit, effort, or reason.

The three brothers represent the three central aspects of human nature. Plato argued that man's nature is composed of three components: intellect/reason, experience/emotion, and conscience/morality. He argued that the highest aspiration of the intellect is truth; of the senses, beauty; and of the soul, goodness. C. S. Lewis later developed this Platonian concept from a biblical perspective in *The Abolition of Man*, employing a head, stomach, and chest metaphor. He asserted that God has made people in a trinitarian form: rational, emotional, and moral. The head represents a person's God-given rationality and restraint, the stomach represents their God-given passions, and the chest represents their moral center—their capacity for both magnanimity and sentiment because they have been made in God's image. Lewis argues that only when a person acknowledges all three aspects of their personhood and yields them to God can they live in right relationship with God and other people.

Dostoyevsky's Dmitri, the eldest son, is clearly intended to represent sensuality, the corruption of passion. He is a man of the earth who seeks money and the gratification of sensory experience. The second son, Ivan, represents the intellect that seeks to find a rational construct. As he says, "The mind I have is a Euclidean, earthbound one, and so how are we to make inferences about that which is not of this world?" He denies a world beyond temporal boundaries. He aspires to employ reason to sort things out—to find a rational, reasonable way of grasping and understanding humanity's significance and purpose. He attempts to solve the human dilemma through a harmonious social structure that anticipates socialism, where people are given bread at the expense of their own freedom and in complacency abandon their desire for freedom. In essence, he would assert a type of divinity by attempting to know the world through reason and apart from God. The third son, Alyosha, represents the soul, or the human spirit. Like the soul/conscience, he plays the role of a mediator throughout the novel, illustrating the necessary and vital relationship of the soul as mediator between mind and body.

Together the three of them present a composite hero, symbolic of the fragmentation of life in a fallen world. Each is forced to endure his own unique form of suffering in order to recognize his hopeless fragmentation. Ivan's denial of God and deification of intellect parallel the arrogance and quest for knowledge that led to the fatal temptation in the garden of Eden. Dmitri's depravity and then overwhelming shame before the prosecutors during his trial poignantly illustrate the effects of sin and rebellion against God. He has indulged his physical urges, yet without any actual gratification. Alyosha, too, is metaphorically implicated in original sin in his lapse of faith in God in the face of diabolic temptation, although he serves the all-important function of showing how the moral component ideally guides and restrains the other two. His momentary lapse in faith leaves his father unprotected. So, all three sons symbolize the fallen human condition, and all of them, in one way or another, are implicated in their father's death.

The character of Smerdyakov serves as a foil to the three brothers. This is seen very clearly in that he offers a hideously distorted mirror image of all three: part person, part parody; part human, part specter; part servant, part master. He is both a son and not a son of Fyodor, both a brother and not a brother of the three legitimate sons. Figuratively, in his speech he is a master of evasiveness and ambiguity. Nowhere is this more evident than in the dialogues with Ivan in which he convinces Ivan that he is the real murderer. Smerdyakov tells him, "I did it with you alone, sir; you and I together murdered him, sir . . . So I want this evening to provide to you and to your face that the principal murderer in it all is exclusively you." In him we grasp the ugly and alienated condition of the human race.

Favorite Passages

I have many favorite passages, although there is space to share only a few. A passage I have found helpful and significant in my own life is one that conveys Alyosha's passion for life: "I want to live for immortality, and I will accept no half-way compromise." He recognizes that it is the metaphysical realm of the soul that offers meaning to human existence in the temporal world. In his quest to live life in view of eternity, he submits himself to the father figure of Zosima, completely resigning his own will to the will of the elder. In Russian Orthodoxy an elder was believed to be one who took another's soul into his soul—another's will into his will. When a man chose an elder, he renounced his own will and yielded in complete submission, complete self-abnegation, in the hope of self-conquest and freedom—freedom from the self. While this mystical element of Russian Orthodoxy is not biblical, it hints at biblical truth. Theologian A. W. Tozer expressed the truth of humanity's struggle in a passage in his book *The Pursuit of God*: "The pronouns "my" and "mine" look innocent enough in print, but their constant and universal use is significant. They express the real nature of the old Adamic man better than a thousand volumes of theology could do. They are verbal symptoms of our deep disease. . . . It would seem that there is within each of us an enemy which we tolerate at our peril. . . . The only effective way to destroy this foe: It is by the Cross. 'Let him take up his cross and follow me'" ([Radford, VA: Wilder Publications, 2008], 18–19). We see such passion in Alyosha's desire to follow the elder, whom he idealizes as a representation of Christ.

Father Zosima makes some very compelling statements that clearly establish him as a Christ type. A sense of the love of Christ is conveyed when he says, "Be not afraid, and never be afraid, and do not be in misery. Just as long as repentance does not grow scarce within you—then God will forgive anything. And indeed there is and can be no sin upon all the earth that the Lord will not forgive the truly repentant." He reminds Alyosha that submission and repentance are his only duties; God does all the rest. Through him Dostoyevsky presents a theme of active and genuine love.

There is a marvelous text that shows the contrast between knowledge about God and faith in God. The elder is engaged in a conversation with a woman who confesses that she is in distress. Fearing that immortality may be fiction and death may be final, she asks how an afterlife can be proved. The elder responds, "How can it be proven, how can one be convinced it is true? . . . By the experience of active love. . . . In the degree to which you succeed in that love, you will also be convinced of God's existence and of your soul's immortality." He then continues to relate the story of a man who once said, "I love mankind . . . but I marvel at myself: the more I love mankind in general, the less I love human beings in particular." Father Zosima continues, "I regret I can say nothing more cheerful to you, for in comparison to fanciful love, active love is a cruel and frightening thing. Fanciful love thirsts for a quick deed, swiftly accomplished, and that everyone should gaze upon it. In such cases the point really is reached where people are even willing to give their lives just as long as the whole thing does not last an eternity but is swiftly achieved, as on the stage, and as long as everyone is watching and praising. Active love, on the other hand, involves work and self-mastery, and for some it may even become a whole science." Here Dostoyevsky establishes a concept of a love that is alive and active, as opposed to a kind of theoretical love often associated with intellectualism and those illusory philosophies that deny the fallen nature of humanity. He reminds his reader that love is only possible through God, not apart from him.

Central Conflicts and Issues

One of the striking aspects of this novel is the anticipation of totalitarian states based on illusory philosophies of an idealized humanity. Dostoyevsky foresaw that this, in fact, would inevitably lead to the oppression of people and destructive ruin of society, as later affirmed by the events of the twentieth century—the bloodiest in human history. This destruction was empowered by the totalitarian ideologies of existentialism, Marxism, and national socialism. These misguided philosophies produced societies where all freedom was lost and life was regarded as cheap—all in the name of an idealized and humanitarian vision. Why? Each of these worldviews elevates the human to divine status and entrusts the person with self-governance while eradicating all absolute foundations for moral behavior. The lessons of classical tragedy and biblical truth were forgotten: humanity is incapable of self-restraint. Hubris is the endemic condition of humanity; catastrophe is the inevitable consequence of such arrogance; redemption through Christ's sacrificial death and resurrection offers the only cure.

Another passage relates the implications of a worldview that eliminates belief in God:

> He [Ivan] solemnly declared in the course of argument that in all the earth there is nothing whatever to compel human beings to love their fellows, and that a law of the type 'man shall love mankind' is wholly non-existent, and that if hitherto there has been any love upon the earth it has proceeded not from a natural law but solely from the fact that human beings have believed in their own immortality. . . . If one were to destroy mankind's faith in its own immortality, there would instantly grow enfeebled within it not only love, but

every vital force for the continuation of universal life. Not only that: then nothing would be immoral, all things would be lawful, even anthropophagy. . . . For every private individual—such as ourselves at present, for example—who believes neither in God nor in his own immortality, the moral law of nature must instantly be transformed into the complete opposite of the old, religious law, and that selfish egoism even to the point of evil-doing must not only be lawful to man, but must even be acknowledged to be necessary, the most reasonable and indeed possibly the most decent way out of the situation.

In response Dmitri cries, "Pardon me . . . just in order to make sure my ears did not deceive me. The argument is as follows: 'Evil-doing must not only be lawful, but even recognized as being the most necessary and most intelligent way out of the situation in which every atheist finds himself!'" Here Dostoyevsky provides his reader with a clear presentation of the central theme of both *Crime and Punishment* and *The Brothers Karamazov*. In the absence of God, and therefore any immutable, absolute standard, all things become permissible. The frightening world of the existentialist is a world where human will and whims, not law or conscience, rule. Such a world is inevitably characterized by power, oppression, selfishness, and cruelty.

Alyosha then stands as the contrast between such a world and the kingdom of God. Alyosha faces a spiritual struggle when he is given a prophecy of future suffering. Yet Father Zosima encourages him, "Cherish him and he will cherish you. You will behold great woe and in that woe you will be happy." He says, "In woe seek happiness." And so, Alyosha's life teaches the principle that through enduring suffering in submission to Christ, true joy is attainable. Alyosha's life demonstrates that love, not power, offers hope to a hurting world.

Dmitri's conflict involves a tremendous discord between sexuality and Eros. This is most clearly described when Dmitri says, "Beauty is a terrifying and a horrible thing!" He is obsessed with beauty and often quotes poetry, but he is confused by the difference between beauty and sensuality. He laments, "The horror of it is that beauty is not only a terrifying thing—it is also a mysterious one. In it the Devil struggles with God, and the field of battle is the hearts of men." Dmitri's struggle illustrates a battle that rages inside all of unredeemed humanity. There is a tragic temptation in unregenerate humanity to seek fulfillment in God's gifts rather than in God himself. This futile quest leads to the worship of gifts, such as beauty, without the enjoyment of them. As the pagan philosopher Plato noted, beauty, truth, and goodness are the highest aspirations of humanity. Yet they are unattainable apart from relationship with God, who created all beauty and exists as ultimate goodness and truth. As the writer of Ecclesiastes and C. S. Lewis asserted, a person cannot find meaning in that which is secondary unless they seek first the primary—the kingdom of God. God's created world and all that it contains provide evidence of him and his love for us; however, he is our actual desire, whether we grasp that concept or not.

I believe the most artistic and controversial section of the novel to be the chapter concerning the Grand Inquisitor. Here Ivan rejects God and, therefore, real love. Ivan says, "This world of God's—I don't accept it, even though I know that it exists, and I don't admit its validity in any way. It isn't God I don't accept, you see; it's the world created by Him, the world of God I don't accept and cannot agree to accept." He goes on to say, "I have never been able to understand how it is possible to love one's neighbor. In my opinion the people it is impossible to love are precisely those near to one, while one can really love only those who are far away." He argues that this idealized love is not realistic or possible. He continues, "It's also possible to love one's neighbor in the abstract, and even sometimes from a distance, but almost never when he's close at hand." He adds, "Actually, people sometimes talk about man's 'bestial' cruelty, but that is being terribly unjust and offensive to the beasts: a beast can never be as cruel as a human being, so artistically, so picturesquely cruel." Dostoyevsky uses Ivan's observations to address some common complaints by religious skeptics. Ivan attempts to use the existence of evil as evidence for God's nonexistence because what he sees in human nature is so vile, so contrary to what he believes would have been established by a loving God. He struggles with this and, at the same time, seeks to reject the idea of original sin because he views children as innocent.

Ivan uses the sufferings of children as his primary challenge to the idea of a good and just God. He says, "I want
rather to be left with sufferings that are unavenged. Let me
rather remain with my unavenged suffering and unassuaged
indignation, even though I am not right. And in any case,
harmony has been overestimated in value, we really don't
have the money to pay so much to get in. And so I hasten to
return my entry ticket." Ivan rejects God, in part, because
he cannot reconcile evil with the existence of a good and
omnipotent deity. Yet his logic is grievously flawed. His very
recognition of evil and suffering suggests a knowledge of an
objective standard. He observes that beasts are incapable of
the cruelty demonstrated by humankind. In both of these
observations, he attacks his own assertions. If a person were
merely a beast, they would live without moral conflict or
knowledge that the world is an unjust place. If good did not
exist in some ideal form, Ivan could have no recognition of a
skewed or perverted good. He seeks to deny or blame God
for a world of suffering and evil while he would elevate to a
divine status the very will that makes evil possible. Through
Ivan, Dostoyevsky cleverly refutes the standard argument of
the skeptic that would both embrace the sovereignty of will
yet denounce God for failing to step in and eradicate evil, a
step that would require the elimination of free will.

Ivan then discusses a poem he has developed called "The
Grand Inquisitor," an allusion to the Inquisition in Seville in
the sixteenth century, some eight centuries after the church
decided to usurp the role of temporal authority. In his poem,
Jesus arrives in Seville during the Spanish Inquisition, just

after many heretics have been burned at the stake. Jesus begins to heal people but is quickly arrested. He is then brought before the Inquisitor, who recognizes him and asks, "Is it you? You? . . . No, do not reply, keep silent. And in any case, what could you say? . . . I do not know who you are, and I do not want to know: you may be He or you may be only His likeness, but tomorrow I shall find you guilty and burn you at the stake as the most wicked of heretics."

The Inquisitor explains that people have brought their freedom and laid it humbly at the feet of the church. He continues, "No science will give them bread while yet they are free, but the end of it will be that they will bring us their freedom and place it at our feet and say to us: 'Enslave us if you will, but feed us.'" Here Dostoyevsky critiques the church's lust for power and its attempts to become the state. His Inquisitor argues, "And all of it again in the name of freedom! I tell you, man has no preoccupation more nagging than to find the person to whom that unhappy creature may surrender the gift of freedom with which he is born." His assertion is that people cannot handle the gift of freedom:

> We corrected your great deed and founded it upon miracle, mystery and authority. And people were glad that they had once been brought together into a flock and that at last from their hearts had been removed such a terrible gift, which had brought them so much torment. . . . We are not with you, but with him, there is our secret! We have long been not with you, but with him, eight

centuries now. It is now just eight centuries
since we took from him that which you in
indignation rejected, that final gift he offered
you, when he showed you all the kingdoms
of the world.

The Inquisitor declares, "Well, we took the sword of Caesar,
and, of course, in taking it rejected you and followed him. . . .
For only we, we, who preserve the mystery, only we shall be
unhappy."

The account ends:

> When the Inquisitor falls silent, he waits for
> a certain amount of time to hear what his
> Captive will say in response. He finds His
> silence difficult to bear. He has seen that the
> Prisoner has listened to him all this time with
> quiet emotion, gazing straight into his eyes
> and evidently not wishing to raise any objec-
> tion. The old man would like the Other to say
> something to him, even if it is bitter, terrible.
> But He suddenly draws near to the old man
> without saying anything and quietly kisses him
> on his bloodless, ninety-year-old lips. That
> is His only response. The old man shudders.
> Something has stirred at the corners of his
> mouth; he goes to the door, opens it and says
> to Him: "Go and do not come back . . . do not
> come back at all . . . ever . . . ever!' And he
> releases him into 'the town's dark streets and
> squares." The Captive departs.
> "And the old man?"

"The kiss burns within his heart, but the old man remains with his former idea."

Using this very vivid imagery, Dostoyevsky refutes the idea of socialism and its longing for a secular order. This passage is not merely his condemnation of the ambitions of the Catholic Church; he also points to the loss of freedom inherent in a socialist context. Furthermore, the passage depicts the human tendency to seek comfort, security, and power rather than true freedom through submission to Christ.

Dostoyevsky then draws a parallel between the three ecclesiastical forces of "miracle, mystery and authority" spoken of by the Grand Inquisitor, the temptations of Christ, and the temptations of the three Karamazov brothers. Christ's first temptation, to turn stone into bread, echoes the dilemma of Dmitri, who seeks sensory gratification. The second temptation of allegiance or authority relates to Ivan's longing for a secular order in which harmony is imposed by force, ultimately, an adumbration of a socialist order. The third temptation, for Jesus to put God to the test by throwing himself off the temple roof, corresponds to the crisis of faith that Alyosha experiences when his deceased mentor is not miraculously preserved from decomposition.

I want to comment on how each of the three brothers symbolically answers the allegations of the Grand Inquisitor. The first answer comes from Alyosha's Cana of Galilee experience, through which we are reminded that we need spiritual regeneration far more than physical sustenance.

Jesus' miracle of turning water into wine demonstrates the new life he offers to those who would receive him. Next, Dmitri provides the second answer. Despite his passionate nature, love of money, and desire to kill his father, he finds inner strength to overcome that passion. Ultimately, through his unjust imprisonment he learns of the collective responsibility of all people for the human condition and discovers salvation through Christ. Ivan supplies the third answer to the Grand Inquisitor's accusations. Ivan confesses to the murder. Those who would say that everything is permitted find they cannot live with the logical implications of that proposition, as it is self-defeating. Ivan's answer is not intellectual but rather derives from his whole being. It is an answer that actually combines the mind, the will, the emotions, the body, the soul, and the spirit. He acknowledges his need. A complete person is revealed in the polyphonic answer of these brothers. Those who were formerly fragmented begin to find faith and reality through suffering—although Ivan's madness is not completely resolved in the plot.

Dostoyevsky used the sequence with the Grand Inquisitor as an ideological prelude to the redemption sequences. The real hero is the Spirit of God working through the characters themselves. At the very end of the novel, there is a triumphal sense of the affirmation and confession of faith in the resurrection: "Karamazov, . . . is it really true what religion says, that we shall all rise up from the dead and come to life and see one another again, and everyone, even Ilushechka?" He is speaking here about a boy who has just died. Alyosha answers, "Without question we shall rise, without question we shall see one another and joyfully tell one another everything that has happened." And so, we see Alyosha moving his ministry into the world, having finally found his place in that world.

Symbolism

I am fascinated by the symbolism of the novel, particularly in the proper names of the key characters. I mentioned earlier that the name of the town in the story actually means "cattle pen." In keeping with this image, Smerdyakov's name means "stinking abomination"; Alyosha's name suggests Alexi, which means "man of God"; and the sensual Dmitri's name derives from the name of the Greek god of corn and fertility. The name Ivan is the Russian form of John, meaning "God is gracious"; and Father Zosima's name in the Greek language suggests life, which relates to the spiritual life that he embodies. Dostoyevsky used coincidence, symbolism, and myth to convey his themes on a variety of levels.

The brothers represent three kinds of human knowledge: physical experience in Dmitri, intellectual reason in Ivan, and intuitive faith in Alyosha. Each encounters a vision and pain, which ultimately lead to redemption. For example, following Alyosha's lapse of faith, he experiences a dreamlike vision in which he hears someone expounding on Jesus' first miracle at Cana of Galilee, the transformation of the water into wine. Simultaneously, he begins to hear another voice, as well: "And you too, my quiet fellow, you too, my meek boy, you too have given this day an onion to a woman who hungered for it [i.e., an onion is being used as a symbol of a valuable gift given to another person]. Begin, dear fellow, begin, meek one, your task! . . . And do you see our sun, do you see it?" Alyosha then whispers, "I'm afraid. . . . I dare not look." The voice continues, "Do not be afraid of it. It is terrible in its greatness before us, dreadful in its loftiness, but it is infinitely merciful, as assumed our likeness and with us is merry and gay, turns water into wine, that the joy of the guests be not broken off, awaits new guests, calls ever new ones and will do so until the end of the ages. Here they come, bring new wine, you see, they are bringing the vessels."

The passage continues,

> "Something was burning in Alyosha's heart, something suddenly filled him to the point of physical pain, tears of ecstasy burst from his soul . . . He stretched out his arms, uttered a scream and awoke. . . . The earth's mystery came into contact with that of the stars. . . . Alyosha stood, looked and suddenly cast himself down upon the earth. . . . Something that was almost an idea took mastery of his intellect—and now for the rest of his life and until the end of the ages. A feeble youth had he fallen to the earth, yet now he arose a resolute warrior for the rest of his life and knew and felt this suddenly, at that same moment of his ecstasy.

The chapter concludes with Alyosha weeping and kissing the earth, comprehending that he is to "abide in the world." "'Someone visited my soul in that hour,' he would say later with resolute faith in his words." Alyosha finally comprehends that it is relationship, not mere religion, that is conveyed in the new wine image of his vision. Dostoyevsky uses this passage to reaffirm that neither organized religion nor reformed political systems can change the soul of humanity—only a visitation by the God of the universe himself can produce such transformation.

Theme: John 12:24

In the preface of *The Brothers Karamazov*, Dostoyevsky dedicated this work to his wife, Anna, and then he quoted from John 12:24. I believe it is impossible to understand this novel without grasping the significance of this Scripture, for it illuminates the central theme: "Truly, truly, I say to you, unless a grain of wheat falls into the earth and dies, it remains alone; but if it dies, it bears much fruit." The Bible clearly teaches that new life is possible only through the death of the old nature. Christ did not come to reform humans; he came to bring new life. This is Paul's message in Galatians 2:20: "I have been crucified with Christ; and it is no longer I who live, but Christ lives in me; and the life which I now live in the flesh I live by faith in the Son of God, who loved me and gave Himself up for me." The brokenness and fragmentation of the human condition can be redeemed only through

Christ's active love. It is not theoretical at all. This love explodes in and through us as we surrender and continue to die to self and live in Christ daily. Even though the author felt that his novel was incomplete, it vividly describes the triumphal movement away from fragmentation, disorder, cacophony, and injustice to wholeness, order, harmony, and justice through salvation and sanctification.

The three dreams (of which we looked at one) appear to represent divine interventions that lead the brothers on their unique paths to redemption. It is through the dreams that they begin to understand that all circumstances can serve to move them toward embracing the truth that they are not our own—that they have been created for a loving purpose. To quote A. W. Tozer again, this is the doctrine of "prevenient grace, which briefly stated means this, that before a man can seek God, God must first have sought the man" (Tozer, *The Pursuit of God*, 11). The Karamazov brothers serve to illustrate God's pursuit of us, in order that he might love us and remake our broken natures.

Although even as a Christian, I experience brokenness and fragmentation day by day, I also experience the power of the indwelling Holy Spirit (Romans 8), who gives me victory, hope, a future, and an assurance that God himself will right all things. As the apostle Paul expressed in the seventh chapter of Romans, "I find then the principle that evil is present in me, the one who wants to do good. For I joyfully concur with the law of God in the inner man" (vv. 21–22). But I also rejoice as Paul rejoices in Romans 7:25: "Thanks be to God through Jesus Christ our Lord!"

The Brothers Karamazov inflames in me a desire for God's kingdom, when Christ will come and reign and deliver us from the corporate unrighteousness from which we cannot extricate ourselves. Christ will again invade human history. In the meantime, we are called to be a people who walk by faith in what the Lord has done, in the hope of what he will do, and in love during this intervening period. As we await the fullness of our redemption, we are called to walk in faith, hope, and love.

Lord, I thank you for this novel, and I pray that you would cause us to be a people who love you and who recognize that we are not here for our happiness, but for our holiness and your glory. We are not here for our comfort, but you have called us to mature in character. I pray that we will pursue that which you have called us to pursue. I thank you for the faith, hope, and love that you have given us in Christ and for the joy that he gives us as we walk with him. We pray in his name. Amen.

NOTES

NOTES

[The Imitation of Christ]

Introduction

The Imitation of Christ belongs to a wonderful tradition of devotional literature that is particularly relevant to the church in times of social upheaval and cultural shallowness—and ours is certainly one of those shallow times in cultural history, not unlike first-century Rome. This book invites us to reflect on some key Christian truths that have been overlooked lately and that challenge virtually all the assumptions of our culture. This is the difficulty and the value of reading a book such as this. Contemporary readers may be shocked by the potency, the clarity, and the pungency of the biblical truths that we have dismissed in order to make the gospel culturally palatable. Since this book predates the Enlightenment, it provides a perspective on truth rarely heard today.

One of the qualities I particularly love about Thomas à Kempis is the way he expressed his clear, sharp mind in combination with his passionate heart. He was both a scholar and a mystic, who provided us with practical exercises and personal devotions. He focused on the importance of simplicity in life, moderation, and disregard for possessions. He also focused on the peace of heart and mind that only the continual presence of God can provide.

The main principle of this book is that practicing the presence of God ushers us into a life of peace and comfort, even in the midst of problems, change, and turmoil. *The Imitation of Christ* invites us to sink our well deep in the rock—deep enough to be nourished by the water of God's Word—so that we can enjoy a settled, accurate, and worshipful view of God.

The enduring power of this book is evidenced by the fact that it has gone through some six thousand editions since it was written in 1471. This remarkably popular book has universal appeal, for it directly and powerfully addresses the problem of human frailty and humanity's struggle with sin. Although cultures change, human nature does not, and so we face the same problems today as those living when Thomas à Kempis wrote it—gossip, harsh criticism, adversity, spiritual dryness, and motivation. He covers these issues and many others in this very practical book.

Imitation is centered on the person of Christ and his work on the cross; therefore, Thomas identified discipleship as believers taking up their own crosses in order to follow Christ. His own burning and abiding love for God is evident in his profound and articulate reflections. Here was a man who spoke out of personal experience, not mere hearsay. He was no armchair theologian, but rather a practitioner who understood human nature and needs.

Through *The Imitation of Christ*, Thomas à Kempis still proves himself a very trustworthy counselor. Themes concerning the love, mercy, and holiness of God are tempered by an eminently realistic and practical approach to the daily issues of the spiritual life. Thomas emphasized right belief as the key to right behavior. He felt that belief and behavior mutually reinforce one another.

But how do we subordinate human nature to divine grace? How do we deal with the issues of self-discipline and self-sacrifice in our self-focused lives and culture? Thomas invited his readers, individually and corporately, to return to God's assessment of life so that they might avoid judging on the basis of outward appearance, discerning instead what really is true and living under the authority of the One who has come into our midst, the incarnate Christ.

Thomas aspired to restore us to a vision of that which is permanent. He argued that it would be foolish for us to invest or exchange our lives for things that are fleeting, yet he noted that many people have regrettably done just that, discovering too late that their years on this planet were not well spent. In fact, they exchanged their souls for things that could not satisfy in the end. So, Thomas affirmed that we need to focus on those things that are permanent, unseen, and enduring, rather than on those things that are temporary, visible, and passing. *Imitation*, like the Book of James, is packed with convicting principles. James asserted the interconnection between faith and fruit—active obedience in response to truth. Likewise, Thomas used his devotions to remind his reader that wisdom involves the application of truth to daily life.

Indeed, one of the aspects of a classic book is that it will continue to benefit the reader through multiple readings. Believers can profit by reading this book every year, much like Bunyan's *The Pilgrim's Progress*. There are certain books that actually age well with us. In fact, what often happens is that as we mature in perspective, we discover things that we didn't see before. In that way, a good book can become almost a good friend, offering reliable counsel, encouragement, and inspiration.

Also worth mentioning is the wealth of quotes from earlier writers. Throughout, Thomas quoted from Aquinas and Augustine as well from many of the Greek and Latin writers, including Ovid, Seneca, and Aristotle. He was acting like the householder in Matthew 13:52, bringing out treasures both new and old and putting them together for us.

Overview

The book can be metaphorically compared to a marvelous mosaic; we can study individual tiles, and we can also step back and appreciate the entire work. Examining *Imitation*, we discover that it is really four books in one. In fact, it was originally found as separate manuscripts. These four separate books were then combined into one book, which was called

The Imitation of Christ. That title comes from the first chapter of the first book. The first book contains useful reminders for the spiritual life; the second offers suggestions for exploring the inner life; the third, which is the longest, deals with the issue of inner comfort as though Christ is addressing the reader directly; and the fourth book deals with the sacrament of Communion and focuses on the presence of Christ in the Eucharist.

Early Christian writers, from about the fifth century on, taught three methods of becoming more like Christ: the way of purgation, the way of illumination, and the way of contemplation—or the unitive way. The first book of *The Imitation of Christ* deals with the concept of purgation, which involves purifying the soul through renunciation, contrition, and confession of sin. This process gradually brings sin to our awareness.

The process also involves brokenness, which God uses to weaken the dominion of the ego, so that we will transfer our reliance for the soul's well-being from ourselves to Christ alone. The purgative way is a painful, but needful, process of finding Christ's life by losing our own life, also termed "increasing mortification." In this way, we move from anxiety to peaceful trust.

Increasing mortification is a very slow progression. I do not hear much today about self-denial or taking up our cross; however, Jesus spoke of this. So, it would be foolish of us to play the game of text management, where we select only those parts we enjoy while ignoring other parts, foolishly supposing this will give us a clear perspective on Christ's teaching. Such an approach only offers the "Gospel according to me," rather than the Gospel according to Matthew, Mark, Luke, and John.

Wisdom is conforming our thinking to what the Gospels teach, rather than trying to conform the Gospels to what we want them to teach. We must guard against worshiping the God we want instead of the God who is, and there is a real danger in doing just that. When we find ourselves struggling with things that our Lord said, things that the Gospels state, and things that the Epistles communicate, I believe that the problem is not in the text, but in us and in our culture. We are, unfortunately, more embedded in our culture, more children of our times, than we might suppose or otherwise want to admit.

The second path for becoming more like Christ and increasingly consecrated to God was something Thomas termed "the way of illumination." This is discussed in the second book and has to do with internal progression. Here the inward life is emphasized, for as our lives are purged of various sins and distractions, the Holy Spirit brings us to a growing realization and enlightenment of God's sovereignty and presence. He reveals more and more truth as we respond to his loving initiatives to deal with these issues. In this stage, Thomas implies that prayer is less an activity and more of a vital reality that flows out of our being. Prayer becomes a response to relationship, not merely something we do.

Life takes on the aura of the mystery of God as we move toward what is called learned ignorance. In my own view, the best scholars in every discipline are humble enough to admit how little they actually know. Ironically, we probably "know more" when we graduate from college than we will ever know after that. Only with experience do we begin to realize how little we know.

This way of illumination is also characterized by growing love and other-centeredness, as we express the love of God through acts of love and service to others. So, the more we understand Christ, the more we are empowered—through the realization of our security in Christ—to begin to serve other people without expecting reciprocity. We begin to serve people around us in tangible ways because we know that we have already received all things.

I believe that the toughest two arenas in which to express that tangible love are at home and at work, and yet those arenas are where we spend the bulk of our time. Thus, many people are tempted to compartmentalize the spiritual life. This might include studying the Bible, going to church, or giving money to missionaries. Yet, I assert that we will learn more about our spirituality by examining our relationships at home and at work than we will learn from our relationships at church or at a Bible study.

The third way Thomas suggested that we can become more like Christ is the unitive way, or the way of contemplation and abandonment of self to grace. This process, discussed in the third book, involves a growing experiential understanding of the mystery that Jesus summarized so beautifully: "Abide in Me, and I in you" (John 15:4). Similarly, the apostle Paul asserted, "It is no longer I who live, but Christ lives in me" (Galatians 2:20).

So what we see in the first three books of *The Imitation of Christ* is really a development of three paths to a consecrated life: purgation, illumination, and the unitive way. Then the fourth book concludes the discussion by focusing on how that union is expressed in the eucharistic symbolism.

The author's desire, expressed repeatedly in this work, was that God might be at all times glorified in us—that we might rest in God alone above all other goods. In the book, Thomas alluded to Jesus' statement "I do not seek your gift. I seek you." This is a very significant principle. Most of us are taught that the way to intimacy with God is through service to him. I argue, along with Thomas, that God is actually infinitely more interested in who we are than in what we do for him. The call of Scripture is to holiness, not morality. We do not become holy by doing. Holiness is imputed to us through Christ's perfection and through his work on the cross and resurrection. As Paul so clearly explained to the Colossian church, "[God] has reconciled you by Christ's physical body through death to present you holy in his sight, without blemish and free from accusation" (Colossians 1:22 NIV). He further stated in Philippians 2:13 that "it is God who works in [believers] to will and to act according to his good purpose" (NIV). In a world filled with competition, performance reviews, and bottom lines, it is easy to forget that we are saved by faith in Christ's sufficiency, not by sentiment, effort, or morality.

Life Sketch

Born Thomas Hemerken, Thomas became known as Thomas à Kempis because of his birthplace in Kempin, Germany, near Düsseldorf. He was born in 1380 to parents of very humble means. He had an older brother, John, who became a member of the Congregation of the Common Life. This community, formed by Gerhard Groote, emulated the community described in Acts 2:44–45, where "all those who had believed were together and had all things in common; and they began selling their property and possessions and were sharing them with all, as anyone might have need." Although members of this congregation did not take permanent vows, they did communally embrace a rule of life that involved poverty, chastity, and obedience.

At the early age of thirteen, Thomas left his parents' home to go live with his brother in the Congregation of the Common Life in Deventer, Germany. Six years later, in 1399, he moved to the monastery of Mount Saint Agnes, and it was there where he spent the rest of his life. After twelve years of preparation, he took his monastic vows in 1406; and then in 1413, at the age of thirty-three, he was ordained into the priesthood. From that point until his death in 1471, we know that he wrote books, became the "master of novices," kept the chronicle of the monastery, and translated and transcribed the Scriptures by hand. He authored several books, including *Prayers and Meditations in the Life of Christ*, *The Garden of Roses*, and *True Wisdom*. He was regarded as an eloquent preacher and a wise confessor. As far as we know, he left the monastery only two times in all those years, and reflecting on those experiences, he said, "As often as I went out among men, I returned less of a man."

The authorship of *The Imitation of Christ* has come under some debate, mainly because the author did not put his name on it. However, from what I have studied and observed, the internal and external evidence indicates it was written by Thomas à Kempis. There are a number of translations, and the one I have chosen is a carefully crafted edition that seeks to make the book relevant to our time yet still faithful to the text. The work was originally written in Latin, the common language of scholars and monastics in the fifteenth century, and it was first translated into English from the French edition in 1503.

Principal Concepts

The Imitation of Christ provides the reader with many useful instructions for cultivating a vibrant spiritual life. Thomas once wrote, "I would much rather feel profound sorrow for my sins than be able to define the theological term for it." In other words, he was much more concerned that he experienced a doctrine than that he had a full grasp of it. It is easy for a theologian to fall in love with a system of propositions, rather than the person of Christ, who has communicated himself to us; and it is good for us to realize that we are tempted to do that. We must realize that God's character is a deep and profound mystery, and no theological system will be able to encapsulate all of him. We must seek to know him through study of Scripture and through prayer while continually examining our lives to see if our beliefs are evident in our hearts and behavior as well as our minds. If not, our beliefs about God will do us little good.

Thomas firmly asserted, "This is the highest wisdom: to see the world as it truly is, fallen and fleeting; to love the world not for its own sake, but for God's; and to direct all your effort toward achieving the kingdom of heaven." True wisdom, as Jonathan Edwards once put it, is to treat things according to their true value. Thus, the most foolish thing we could do would be to treat the things that are fleeting as though they were lasting and the things that are enduring as insignificant.

This is why Jesus warned us in Luke 16:15, "For that which is highly esteemed among men is detestable in the sight of God." It is very possible for us to invest our lives in those things that God says are utterly futile and worthless. We must discern what the real price tags are according to God's perspective. As Thomas wrote, "It is vanity to wish for a long life and to care little about a good life." In other words, a long life isn't as important as a godly life. Frankly, even a very long life is as a breath of air in comparison to eternity. All lives are brief, in this sense, and Thomas stressed again and again the pilgrim nature of our lives here on earth. We are to consider ourselves as sojourners and strangers and aliens.

Thomas then addressed the danger of an excessive thirst for knowledge, warning that it, like all good things, can become an idol and distraction. Therefore, it would be wise, to

be sure, that when we seek knowledge, we also seek application. He advised, "If you want to learn something that will
really help you, learn to see yourself as God sees you and not
as you see yourself in the distorted mirror of your own self-
importance." This is a convicting passage for some of us. If
we are not careful, that distorted mirror of self-importance
will deceive us, and it would be much wiser, Thomas argued,
to see ourselves in light of who God says we are.

In chapter 3, entitled "Of the Teaching of Truth," he wrote,
"All perfection in this life has some accompanying imperfection, and all our speculation is not without some darkening
mist. A humble understanding of yourself is a surer way to
God than a profound searching after knowledge." Again, his
invitation is to self-knowledge, to grasp what God says of our
spiritual condition and to invite the Holy Spirit to search us.
He continued, "Nevertheless, many people have chosen to
seek knowledge rather than to live well, and they are often
led astray and their lives come to very little—or nothing at
all. . . . That person is truly great who has great love. He is
truly great who is small in his own eyes and who regards
every pinnacle of honor as nothing in itself."

In the chapter called "Of Thinking before You Act,"
Thomas noted, "It is sad to say, but we are so weak that we
are more ready to believe bad things about another person—and to spread them around—than we are to believe
or to say something good about them." We haven't changed
much in all these intervening years, have we? Though writing many centuries ago, he understood human nature only
too well. There is something in us that loves to hear bad

reports. That is why the news is so popular and bad news is particularly popular—hence the phrase "If it bleeds, it reads." We may see a few human-interest stories here and there, but what really sells is bad news. I think Thomas was reminding his reader that our criticism of others is a reflection of both our pride and our self-righteousness.

Regarding the reading of spiritual writings, Thomas argued, "Do not ask 'Who said this?' but pay attention to what is said. People pass away, but the truth of the Lord endures forever." He was warning against seeking personal glory and being a respecter of persons based on worldly values. In earlier periods of time, artists and craftsmen typically did not sign their work; they did their work anonymously. This is why there was some controversy as to the authorship of *The Imitation of Christ*—the author didn't sign it.

These artists were attesting that God is the real author of all beauty and that we do not need to seek credit on earth for what we do. We pursue fame to impress people, but Thomas asserted that if we are impressed with success and material things, we will become restless: "The proud and greedy never rest; the poor and humble in spirit rest in great peace."

In a chapter titled "Of Avoiding Empty Hope and Self-Praise," Thomas observed, "Anyone who places all his trust in people or in other created things is foolish. Do not be ashamed to serve others for the love of Jesus Christ and to appear poor in this world." Here he emphasized the virtue of humility. He went on to advise, "If you have any good qualities, believe that other people have better ones; by doing so you will retain your humility. It does you no harm if you place yourself beneath everyone else; it does you great harm, though, if you place yourself above even one other person."

I don't think he was suggesting that we deceive ourselves. He was inviting us to humility and to the realization that without God, we really are nothing, but with him we have all things. The key to humility is not self-deprecation but focusing on God's grace. As we focus on the grace of God, we are then able to take our eyes off ourselves. Frankly, there is a perverse form of humility that actually degrades the self. As long as the focus is on the self, pride is involved. True humility finds itself preoccupied with the surpassing grace God displayed in his indescribable gift of Christ.

In speaking about obedience for those under religious vows, Thomas claimed, "Run here or run there, you will find no peace except in humbly placing yourself under the rule of a Superior." That is an interesting thought. We live in a pioneer culture that has little room for authority. The only authority we embrace is what we ourselves feel and think; however, it is a good discipline to put ourselves under the authority of others, seeking mentors—people we trust to give us guidance as from the Lord. Being accountable to others can prevent us from deceiving ourselves.

In a chapter called "Of Avoiding Unnecessary Talk," Thomas addressed the issue of idle chatter and gossip: "If it is proper to speak, speak of what will benefit others spiritually." Many of us struggle with speaking ill of others by questioning their intentions and motives, especially when we feel insulted by some comment or action. It would be much wiser for us to speak well of others or, if we can't speak favorably, to keep silent.

He then discussed the potential usefulness of troubles in a later chapter: "Sometimes it is good for us to have troubles and hardships, for they often call us back to our own hearts." He was well aware of God's ability to use and redeem adversity, brokenness, and trouble in our lives, understanding that God is powerful enough to use all circumstances to drive us to a greater realization of our desperate need for him. Rather than teaching a simplistic notion of a smooth and easy life in Christ, Thomas promoted a more biblical understanding that God uses the pain and adversity of an imperfect world to draw us ever closer to him. Though a pagan, Euripides once advised, "Do not consider painful what is good for you." That is sound advice. Pain and adversity are but temporary. Ultimately, we are being prepared for a destiny where there will be no tears, no sorrow, and no moaning, crying, or weeping.

In a chapter called "Of Resisting Temptation," Thomas observed, "We have all been born with a fierce, self-centered desire for success, status and pleasure that clashes with our longing for God." He argued that temptation has a way of revealing who we are. Our responses to temptation potentially teach us more about ourselves than our many successes, for we can learn much more about ourselves through failure and setbacks than through our achievements. He further explained, "Some people are spared from great temptations and are often overcome in small daily ones." It is true that there are people who can do very well with the big issues and then become snared by the trivial ones, and Thomas went on to say, "This happens so that, being humbled, they may never trust themselves in great things if they are so weak in such ordinary ones."

He then went on to address the issue of motives with regard to work and achievement, asserting, "God places more importance on the reason you work than on how much work you actually do." This is a very important principle. There should be no dichotomy between the sacred and the secular; Thomas implied that work in the monastery could be secular if men were doing it for the wrong reasons. This concept was developed more fully during the time of Martin Luther, but the central principle is this: that which appears spiritual may not actually be if the focus of the person's heart is on the self instead of on God.

I think that the converse can be true as well. That which seems to be secular may actually be spiritual if the individual is motivated to action by the love of Christ. Even the most mundane, routine task can become extraordinary when done for the sake of the Master, rather than to impress people. This concept is clearly taught in the third chapter of Colossians, and it is something that we all need to grasp. This is why I say that all believers are called to full-time engagement in ministry. Our ministries will manifest themselves in various ways and via large or small arenas of influence; nonetheless, all of us are called to love and serve people for the sake of Christ. The more we become renewed by the truth, the more we are empowered to serve and invest in the lives of other people.

Thomas also wrote of the monastic life, dealing with the concept of being a stranger—a sojourner or pilgrim—on earth. This concept, however, is not limited to the cloister. All of us ought to embrace this mentality, for it is biblical (1 Peter 2:11; Hebrews 11:9–10). In this life, Thomas reminded us, "you have come to serve, not to rule." Someday we will rule with Christ, but presently we serve, and we serve God best when we serve others, realizing that Christ himself did not come to be served. It's as if he says: "If I have so served you, you should also serve one another. If I have loved you, you must love one another. If I have forgiven you, you must forgive one another. If I have embraced you as my friends, you are now to do that with others." Christ invites us to do that which he has already done for us.

In his discussions about religious training, Thomas argued that progress follows intention. This is another important principle. He explained, "The intention of earnest and well-meaning people depends more on the grace of God than on their own wisdom; such people always place their trust in God no matter what they do, for man proposes but God disposes." This echoes the truth expressed in Proverbs 16:9. According to Thomas, "The path a person takes does not lie within himself." Again he reminded us that even our ability to desire to follow God is a gift of grace; we are not self-sufficient. Keeping that in mind, he then exhorted us to examine our inward and outward affairs.

There is a somewhat meddling chapter in *Imitation* called "Of the Love of Solitude and Silence." I call it meddlesome, for we all struggle with this issue because we do not value silence sufficiently. In fact, our modern society seems to exhibit almost a fear of silence, avoiding it at all costs. We have iPods, ever-present cell phones, in-car DVD players, and ubiquitous televisions. Furthermore, our conversation often tends toward the trivial. Warning of this, Thomas observed that there is a danger of losing our perspective, our cutting edge, "when we have spent a long time in idle chatter." He suggested that our lives can be enriched and enlivened by silence: "No one leads securely except the person who freely serves. No one commands securely except the person who thoroughly obeys. No one knows secure joy except the person who holds a good conscience in his own heart." He recommended that we need to draw close "to a person who seeks solitude and silence."

The Bible repeatedly affirms the importance of listening, which typically requires silence. Samuel heard God's voice and command in the stillness of the night and was able to respond to his call. Similarly, Elijah was able to hear God's words of encouragement when he was removed to the wilderness, where God ministered to him. In fact, God revealed himself rather remarkably. The text tells us that Elijah first observed a great wind, then an earthquake, and then a fire, but God was in none of these. Finally, there came a gentle whisper, and through this subtle means, God spoke to his prophet (1 Kings 19). Psalm 46:10 commands, "Be still, and know that I am God" (NIV). All of these passages, and many more that I have not specifically noted, highlight the necessity of silence so that we might hear God speaking. Unfortunately, silence has become uncomfortable to us is our frenetic society. We equate it with boredom and loneliness. In contrast, Thomas (and Scripture) links silence with solitude and receptivity.

Despite the difficulty inherent in setting aside times of solitude, it is vital that we discipline ourselves to designate both time and place to study and pray, as well as to listen to what God then has to say to us.

The Imitation of Christ also includes a chapter on death, in which Thomas proposed, "You ought to master yourself in every act and thought as if you were to die today." According to Thomas, purposeful living has much to do with an accurate perspective on the brevity of life and the goal of the pilgrimage. If we remain mindful of the fact that we could die tonight, won't we be more likely to live deliberately in the moment, knowing it could be our last? This concept is beautifully illustrated in one of Shakespeare's plays, *Hamlet*. Near the end of the story, Hamlet suspects two other characters are conspiring to kill him, yet he confidently asserts God's sovereignty when he alludes to Matthew 24, saying, "There is a special providence in the fall of a sparrow. If it [death] be now, 'tis not to come; if it be not to come, it will be now; if it be not now, yet it will come. The readiness is all" (V, ii). What Hamlet means is this: death is certain, whether it be imminent or distant. Because we cannot know when death will come, we must live purposefully in the moment, confident of God's care for us and ready to stand before him when our time comes. Truly, the readiness is all!

Shifting topic a bit, Thomas also observed that by watching out for those things that irritate us in other people, we can become aware of the same habits in ourselves. I have found this to be true. I often learn more about myself in what irritates and annoys me in other people than I might want to suppose; the things that really bother me about other people are frequently very true about me as well. Instead of reacting to others with anger, I try to ask myself if this is an invitation to self-understanding and then consider why that habit bothers me so much in others.

The way we react to others is often a projection of what is going on in us, so even well before the age of psychology, here was a man who understood something of intrapersonal dynamics. There are three powerful dynamics that make it possible for us to deceive ourselves in boundless ways: denial, rationalization, and projection. We tend to perceive the world from our own point of view, we deny that we have done anything wrong by rationalizing or excusing our bad behavior, and we project onto or attribute to others our own unacceptable attitudes. I know this is quite theoretical, but I believe that we use these capacities to deceive ourselves. As far back as the fifteenth century, Thomas understood these defense mechanisms.

Because he understood self-deception, he promoted the development of a rich inner life and advocated self-examination:

> We cannot trust ourselves too much, because we often lack grace and understanding. The light in us is small, and we soon let even this burn out for lack of care. Moreover, we often fail to notice how inwardly blind we are; for example, we frequently do wrong, and to make matters worse, we make excuses about it! Sometimes we are moved by passion and

think it zeal. We condemn small things in others and pass over serious things in ourselves. We are quick enough to feel it when others hurt us—and we even harbor those feelings—but we do not notice how much we hurt others. A person who honestly examines his own behavior would never judge other people harshly.

In other words, the more we grasp what we are really like, in our heart of hearts, the slower we will be to condemn other people for those same weaknesses. Thomas advised, "An inward person puts the care of his own soul before all other cares, and a person who attends to himself does not gossip about others. You will never be inward and devout unless you stop talking about other people and start watching over yourself."

He then went on to encourage the joy of a good conscience: "The person who has great peace of heart pays no attention to either praise or blame." This is a difficult issue for many of us. I know it is hard for me. I want to listen to praise and blame. I get very, very serious when I hear blame and criticism. And what is my first response? I immediately want to defend myself. And praise, too, can be very distracting. Human beings are the only animal that when you pat them on their backs, their heads swell.

There was an instance not long ago when I was talking with a friend while listening to another conversation of two people talking about me. I pretended not to hear it, but I actually listened carefully to hear what they had to say. You see, my problem is that I am so concerned about the praise and blame of others that I sometimes fail to be concerned about God's view of me. If I fear the opinions of people, I will lose my fear of God. I cannot be focused on impressing people and pleasing God at the same time. I must choose between the two.

Commenting on this, Thomas wrote, "People look at appearances; God looks at the heart. People consider what you have done; God clearly considers your intentions." Again, he was exhorting us to look below the surface, and the best surface to look below is our own. We don't need to deal with what is below the water line of other people; we have enough to deal with regarding our own motivations.

The Imitation of Christ encourages us to "love all things for Jesus' sake, but love Jesus for his own sake." If I can love all things for his sake, then I will be able to receive all things from him and through him and cheerfully give my life and achievements back to him. As Thomas put it, "I wish for no divine comfort that blunts the stab of conscience in my heart, nor do I aspire to a lofty contemplation that may lead to spiritual pride. Not everything high is holy nor everything sweet, good nor every desire, pure nor every affection pleasing to God. I willingly accept that grace which makes me more humble and reverent, more ready to abandon myself into God's hands." He observed that "Jesus has many lovers of his heavenly kingdom these days, but few of them carry his cross. He has many who desire comfort, but few who desire affliction. He has many friends to share his meals, but few to share his fasts. Everyone is eager to rejoice with him but few are willing to endure anything for him."

These are hard words that wouldn't play well in most sermons today, but they are just the words that we need to hear repeatedly. If we are not careful, we will be persuaded by false, feel-good theology rather than truth. Writing as though Jesus were speaking to us, Thomas encouraged, "You should make my will your own, stop being enamored of yourself, and eagerly do what I ask of you. Enthusiasm often drives you to action, but take the time to learn whether what you do is for me or for yourself."

Many times I have engaged in ministry, only to look back and realize that I did it for myself. I realized later that the intention of my heart was selfish. Along these lines, Thomas offered this prayer, "Lord, you know what is best. Let this or that be done as you wish. Give what you want, how much you want and when you want. Do with me as you think best and as best pleases you and in a way which will give you greater honor. Put me where you want me and use me freely. I am in your hand; turn me around whichever way you will."

These are strong and radical prayers, but they are the sort that can move us toward discernment and the realization that we need to submit to God's will, rather than to try to manipulate him into doing our will. May we be able to say with Thomas, "Let your will be mine, and let my will always follow yours and be in perfect accord with it."

Perhaps Thomas's richest statement in *The Imitation of Christ* is this:

> Grant me most sweet and loving Jesus, to
> rest in you above every other creature, above

all health and beauty, above all glory and
honor, above all power and dignity, above
all knowledge and precise thought, above all
wealth and talent, above all joy and exultation,
above all fame and praise, above all sweetness
and consolation, above all hope and promise,
above all merit and desire, above all gifts and
favors you give and shower upon me, above all
the happiness and joy that the mind can understand and feel, and finally, above all angels
and archangels, above all the hosts of heaven,
above all things visible and invisible, and above
all that is not you, my God.

He desired a singular vision and a pure heart. When all
the threads of Thomas's contemplations are woven together,
I think they ultimately invite us to be people who commit
time to study and prayer, solitude and silence, so that we can
grow in spiritual depth. The writer of Hebrews wrote of the
importance of maturing in the faith: "Anyone who lives on
milk, being still an infant, is not acquainted with the teaching
about righteousness. But solid food is for the mature, who
by constant use have trained themselves to distinguish good
from evil. Therefore let us leave the elementary teachings
about Christ and go on to maturity" (5:13–6:1 NIV). So,
let us be people who are careful about what we expose our
minds and hearts to and who are disciplined to live with the
end in view. Let us transcend our own time by not being
infantile or parochial and by exposing ourselves to the truth
of the Word and to the lives of holy men and women who

have gone before us.

Thomas Oden, in his book *Requiem* (1995), wrote that he was becoming a "paleo-orthodox" theologian. What he meant was that he had come to focus on what was the unified vision of the early church up until the period of the Council of Nicaea in 325. Then, there was no Eastern or Western church. There wasn't a Protestant church or Roman Catholic Church or Orthodox church; there was only the one holy, catholic, and apostolic church. There was unified doctrine and understanding. We used to be told, "Don't trust anybody over thirty." Remember that? Oden stated it differently. He said he doesn't trust anybody who is younger than three hundred.

It is prudent to examine pre-Enlightenment supposi-tions and grasp the truth that there is a vision—a "discarded image," as C. S. Lewis described it—that has been lost. It would be advantageous for us to read and expose ourselves to truths that cause us to see things for what they are, rather than what they seem to be. Let us be people who embrace the pilgrimage of life, who realize how brief and ephemeral our lives are, so that we might live wisely and well.

Those who lose their lives in this way will find them for Christ's sake. Those who relinquish the aspirations of the world will actually discover the love and joy and peace that the world constantly seeks. People suppose they want power and position, prestige and popularity. They suppose they want those achievements, but what they really want is what they think those successes will bring—love, joy, and peace. However, love, joy, and peace are the fruit of the Spirit that is produced in us as we seek the Lord above all else. Then the mysterious peace of God that surpasses comprehension will garrison our minds and our hearts as we take the risk of trusting in him, abandoning the illusion of self-sufficiency.

Father, we thank you for this opportunity to think, to reflect, to quiet our hearts before you. May we slow down enough that we begin to consider again those things that matter and those things that last. Thank you for the words of your servant Thomas à Kempis, who, though he is in your presence, still speaks to us. May we be wise enough to listen to these admonitions and encouragements, to the comfort and consolation and counsel of these truths. We pray in Christ's name. Amen.

NOTES

NOTES